DISCOVERING
Jesus

A study for learning about Jesus, who He is, and what He has done for me.

Hermie Reynolds

5 Fold Media
Visit us at www.5foldmedia.com

Discovering Jesus
Copyright © 2014 by Hermie Reynolds
Published by 5 Fold Media, LLC
www.5foldmedia.com

All rights reserved. No part of this book may be reproduced, stored in a retrieval system, or transmitted in any form or by any means-electronic, mechanical, photocopy, recording, or otherwise-without prior written permission of the copyright owner, except by a reviewer who wishes to quote brief passages in connection with a review for inclusion in a magazine, website, newspaper, podcast, or broadcast. Cover imagery © Leonid Ikan-Fotolia.com. The views and opinions expressed from the writer are not necessarily those of 5 Fold Media, LLC.

Unless otherwise identified, Scripture quotations are taken from the New King James Version. Copyright © 1982 by Thomas Nelson, Inc. Used by permission. All rights reserved.

Scripture quotations marked AMP are taken from the Amplified® Bible. Copyright © 1954, 1958, 1962, 1964, 1965, 1987 by The Lockman Foundation. Used by permission.

Scripture quotations marked NLT are taken from the Holy Bible, New Living Translation, copyright 1996, 2004. Used by permission of Tyndale House Publishers., Wheaton, Illinois 60189. All rights reserved.

Scripture quotations marked MSG are taken from *THE MESSAGE*. Copyright © by Eugene H. Petersen 1993, 1994, 1995, 1996, 2000, 2001, 2002. Used by permission of NavPress Publishing Group.

Scripture quotations marked TLB are taken from The Living Bible; Tyndale House, 1997, © 1971 by Tyndale House Publishers, Inc. Used by permission. All rights reserved.

Scripture quotations marked TPT are taken from *Luke: to the Lovers of God, The Passion Translation*™, copyright © 2012. Used by permission of 5 Fold Media, LLC, Syracuse, NY 13039, United States of America. All rights reserved.

ISBN: 978-1-936578-98-6

Library of Congress Control Number: 2014944782

Dedication

Thank you, Father God, for allowing me to write a book about Your Son, Jesus. I dedicate this book to You, Jesus. I am forever grateful for what You have done for me!

This book is dedicated to all the pastors and Bible teachers who have ministered to me and imparted into my life. I am thankful for the many different ministries that God has connected me with through the years. Some have imparted into my life through books, messages on CD, or the Internet. Thank you for all your hard work! I dedicate this book to every person who has laid down their lives to share the message of Jesus Christ.

Thank you to Andy and Cathy Sanders and 5 Fold Media who have been such a great help to guide me through the publishing process with *Discovering God* and *Discovering Jesus*.

Thank you to my wonderful family and prayer partners; without your support, writing this book would not have been possible.

Endorsements

"*Discovering Jesus* is the second installment of a journey to know God better. Hermie gives herself in an unusual way to the study of God. She approaches the study of Scripture with a devotional heart and an academic zeal. This relentless search for truth has led her straight into the path of the One who has the keys of life—Jesus, the God-Man. Jesus says that He is the way, the truth, and the life and that no one comes to the Father except through Him. He is the escort to the Father and to the very ways of God. To study Jesus may be the wisest thing one can do.

Hermie has met the Key of Life, and with the heart of a teacher, she has sought to present Him in a stimulating way to beginner and seasoned believers alike. She has again poured her life's study into the pages of the book you are holding.

Someone once said that "it takes Jesus to know Jesus," meaning that Jesus must open the eyes of your heart to truly know Him. Glean from a heart that has been opened as you read, study, and pray through this book. As you do, I believe that a hunger for Jesus, the very Word of God, will rise within you, just as it has for Hermie."

Rusty Geverdt
Founder, Cincinnati House of Prayer
Greater Cincinnati Prayer

"I met Hermie Reynolds several years ago and had the privilege of being her pastor for a time. One cannot know Hermie very long at all without discovering her passion for Jesus and the desire in her heart to make Him known. It is my hope that as you use this delightful and practical resource, you too will discover this Jesus and find that, like Hermie, you are passionate for Him."

Chris Sheneman
Senior pastor, NewSong Vineyard Church

"Hermie wrote her first book, *Discovering God*, with both a God-given gift to write and a faithful and obedient heart. She follows the Lord's leading without knowing what is going to happen next; she is willing to take one step and wait for Him to illuminate the next. It has been exciting to see *Discovering God* take wing and find its way into the hands of people around the world who have discovered God in a new way. The Lord has even used the book inside the prison system and set captives free—unplanned in the beginning by Hermie, but orchestrated by God once the book was published. It is with much expectancy that I wait to see what God has planned for Hermie's second book, *Discovering Jesus*. Hermie's writing brings a depth of insight from the Word interwoven with personal examples that draw readers into the heartfelt story she tells about life in Jesus. I pray for those whose hearts will be touched by *Discovering Jesus* and who will begin a lifelong adventure in Him. To Him be the glory!"

John Gordon
Associate director and pastor
Cincinnati House of Prayer

"One of the last words given by Jesus while on this earth was, "Go therefore and make disciples of all the nations" (Matt 28:19). It is a wonderful thing to see people come to know Christ, but what about the "make disciples" part? Hermie Reynolds' first book, *Discovering God*, laid the foundation for new believers to understand who their Father in heaven is and how to relate to Him. Her new book, *Discovering Jesus*, will do much the same, this time helping the new believer understand who their Lord and Savior is and how to walk with Him. These books are great resources to have in your personal library and to share with a friend or new believer."

Jeff Maglich
Co-pastor, Oxford Vineyard Church

"It is said that in the Hebrew language there is no word for *coincidence*. The belief is that when people meet it is by the divine direction of God. Approximately three years ago I met Hermie Reynolds at the Cincinnati House of Prayer. I was introduced to Hermie by my wife, Regina. Hermie Reynolds is an anointed and chosen vessel of the Lord. God has called her "for such a time as this." It's been approximately three years since prophetically by the Spirit of the Lord I saw Hermie writing multiple books and God making her name a household name in the body of Christ. How the Lord has honored His people as He has launched the ministry of Hermie Reynolds. I believe prophetically this book, *Discovering Jesus,* is the second book in the first trilogy written by Hermie. God has gifted her to communicate His Word by using a vast array of subjects in her books. I pray as you read this book, *Discovering Jesus,* that God will intimately reveal to you the divine purpose of His son (Ephesians 1:17-19)."

Apostle David Porter III
Dunamis Life All Nations Church, Inc.

"You can see a picture, how Jesus looks in daily life by reading *Discovering Jesus*. It is a book full of scriptural truth interspersed with personal stories that keep it very interesting. Those looking for Jesus and those who know Him already can benefit from reading this book. Hermie knows Jesus, and it is clear here."

Susan Courtney
Facilitator for Regional Prophetic Intercessors, Ohio

"Hermie's book gives a strong foundation for young believers to not only know about Jesus but to find Him in a personal way. As Hermie says, 'It is good to ask yourself: who is Jesus to me? What you decide about this man, Christ Jesus, can change your life.'

This book is excellent material for small group discussions. She gives good tips on how to lead discussions based on the material and what to ask regarding each chapter. Hermie's writing style is easy to read—sharing Bible stories and personal examples in a fluent way. Most important, Hermie teaches all about Jesus, who is the most beloved and controversial Person in history."

Sandy Warner
Author of the Quickened Word blog
www.thequickenedword.com

Contents

Foreword	11
Introduction	15
How to Use This Book for Group Discussion	19
Chapter 1: The Promise	21
Chapter 2: Jesus, Gift from Heaven to Earth	33
Chapter 3: Jesus Starts His Ministry	45
Chapter 4: The Teaching of Jesus	55
Chapter 5: The Kingdom of Heaven	67
Chapter 6: Healing the Sick	79
Chapter 7: The Garden of Gethsemane	93
Chapter 8: The Cross	103
Chapter 9: The Blood of Jesus	113
Chapter 10: The Resurrection of Jesus	125
Chapter 11: The Birth of the New Testament Church	135
Chapter 12: Jesus, Returning Bridegroom King	145
Pondering the Word	157

Foreword

I have heard it said through the years I have served the Lord that the greatest challenge that America faces in this hour of history is a lack of the knowledge of God. I couldn't agree more with that statement. We lack a basic understanding of God—who He is, how He operates, what motivates Him, and more. We live in a time when more and more people are questioning the very existence of God while fewer and fewer turn to the Bible for answers to those questions. Our participation in the expressions of the local church in general has decreased while other interests have captured our hearts and have become more relevant than following after a God we don't know or believe even cares about what goes on in our day to day lives on this earth. As a people, we need a Saul encounter on the road to Damascus. We need a John the Revelator encounter that opens the eyes of our understanding to who God really is, to see He does truly exist and that He actually does care about our very existence. We need to discover once again in this generation who God is.

In this book, entitled *Discovering Jesus*, Hermie will take you on a journey of discovery of who the Son of God really is. She will help you see Him—perhaps for the first time.

The word *revelation* means "laying bare" or "disclosure of truth."[1] Revelation, simply put, is to lay bare or make known what was not previously known. When it comes to our lives in relation to God, we need wisdom and revelation to walk in understanding. We need wisdom and revelation to walk and follow God. The apostle Paul prays for it in

---

1. Thayer and Smith, "Greek Lexicon entry for Apokalupsis," The NAS New Testament Greek Lexicon, accessed July 14, 2014, http://www.biblestudytools.com/lexicons/greek/nas/apokalupsis.html.

Ephesians 1:17 when He asks the Lord to give us a spirit of wisdom and revelation so that we may know Him better.

Just like that prayer of Paul's, I believe that today men and women all over the earth are crying out to gain understanding of who God is. Who is this One called Jesus? I believe it is a universal cry of the human heart unto their Creator to look for and long for understanding and knowledge of the One who formed and fashioned them for this life and beyond. I also believe it is the very heart of God to answer that cry and to lay bare, make known, and give revelation to the eyes of our understanding so that we may come to know and discover this One.

In this book, you will discover again or for the first time, the One who came in the flesh to save mankind from the ravages of their sin and wickedness, and to bring man back into relationship with God. You will discover Jesus the Christ! This One who is fully God and fully man, perfect in all His ways. Though He died on the cross, He is alive at the right hand of God the Father in the throne room of heaven where He is ministering in intercession on behalf of the purposes of God on earth and through mankind. He waits for His Father's appointed time to break forth again on the earth to establish His kingdom on earth. He is the One who described Himself to the apostle John in the book of Revelation like this:

"I am the Alpha and the Omega, the Beginning and the End," says the Lord, "who is and who was and who is to come, the Almighty. …I am He who lives, and was dead, and behold, I am alive forevermore. Amen. And I have the keys of Hades and of Death" (Revelation 1:8, 18).

In the book entitled *Who Ate Lunch with Abraham*, author Asher Intrater describes the revelatory importance of seeing Yeshua (Jesus) as He truly is:

"How we see Yeshua affects how we see ourselves. We are made in the image of God (Genesis 1:27). Yeshua is that image of God for us and in us. Those who see themselves as descended from apes will necessarily have a low opinion of human nature. Our origins determine our outcome. We see ourselves not as evolving from apes, but as repenting of our sins and becoming glorified sons of God in the image of Yeshua.

How we see Him is how we see our destiny. With each stage of revelation of who Yeshua is, there is a corresponding development in the revelation of our destiny in Him. We are in Him and He is in us. Each level of identity has a corresponding new level of authority.

The revelation of Yeshua as king of Israel was given to Simeon (Peter) in Matthew 16. Yeshua told Simeon that this revelation was not human or natural, but heavenly and supernatural (verse17). At that moment, Peter received spiritual authority such that whatever he would bind or loose on earth would be done so in heaven (verses18-19). The same is true for anyone today who comes to faith in the same revelation that Simeon Peter had.

The revelation of Yeshua as head of the Church was given to Saul (Paul) in Ephesians 1. Yeshua has ascended into heaven over all powers and principalities (verses 20-21). This understanding was given to Saul by revelation. He prayed for us to have the same enlightenment (verses17-18). That enlightenment will impart to us the same power and authority that Yeshua has, both in this world and the world to come. We are seated with Him spiritually in heaven (Ephesians 2:6-7).

The first stage of our destiny is revealed to us through Peter in the gospels, the second stage through Paul in the epistles. The ultimate stage is through John in the book of Revelation.

As we meditate on the vision of Yeshua in the book of Revelation, a change takes place in us. As we grasp who He really is, so do we grasp who we really are in Him. His eyes are a flame of fire. He wears many crowns. He is dressed in white, with a gold band on His chest and a sword coming out of His mouth. His hair is like wool and His face is shining like the sun.

When that picture gets IN us, it makes us different. Fire comes out of our eyes. There is new power, passion, and purity. Holiness and zeal burns out carnality and worldliness. We see a heavenly perspective of the kingdom. We are made for His coming, and made ready for the spiritual warfare leading up to that coming. Grace is imparted to our souls.

May God grant us the understanding of who Yeshua is as was revealed to Peter, Paul, and John! And may we be changed to be like Him."[2]

Today, perhaps like no other time in history, we need the knowledge of God. We need a revelation that shows us the glory of Jesus Christ. We need to discover again the Son of the living God. This book will help you do just that. As you ask the Lord for revelation of the Son of God in prayer, worship, and study of His Word, I pray this book helps you see and know Him as He is, has been, and will be, so that you may be forever transformed in your own lives.

I believe you are about to discover the Son of God, for the first time or all over again. I pray it is so!

Walter P. Barr
Director and lead pastor of Cincinnati House of Prayer

---

2. Asher Intrater, *Who Ate Lunch with Abraham* (Frederick, MD: Intermedia, 2011), 128-129 www.reviveisrael.org.

Introduction

What comes to your mind if I ask you, "Who is Jesus?" Some people will think of a Christmas scene with baby Jesus in the manger; others will think of Jesus on the cross. It is good to ask yourself, "Who is Jesus to me?" What you decide about this man, Christ Jesus, can change your life. I grew up in church but didn't come into a personal relationship with Jesus until I was twenty-three years old. Before I surrendered my life to Jesus I tried to live a good life, I tried to pray and read my Bible, but it felt like there was a barrier between me and God. I just could not get through to Him. During this time I had a desire to know God personally, but I didn't know how to get there.

Jesus shared a story about the Prodigal Son who squandered his inheritance. His father came running when his son returned. When you have a desire to get to know God, He will go to great lengths to meet you. During this time when I was searching for answers to my problems, a friend invited me to a Bible study. I was twenty-three years old and the book we studied had three circle diagrams on the page. Inside every circle were the things of life that occupy our time—house, family, work, television, reading, etc. In the first picture Jesus was outside the circle. In the second picture Jesus was in the circle, one of the many things that occupy my time. In the last circle Jesus was on the throne in the middle of the circle and all the other things had lesser importance. The question was: which one of these three circles represented my life? I knew where Jesus should be, and He was not there, so that day I surrendered my life to Jesus and put Him in the first place, the most important place in my life.

Discovering God and *Discovering Jesus* were birthed out of the need I saw in young believers who were hungering to know God more and did not know where to start in this journey. I also saw the struggles my kids went through during high school and realized that without strong foundations, they would not make it through the challenges they were facing. There were so many things that they encountered that were not in agreement with the truth of the Bible. A simple dream set me on the journey to study and teach about the attributes of God, and that was followed by a "Who is Jesus?" class. To my surprise, I found that my faith grew stronger. No longer did I base what God would do for me on my performance, but my focus shifted to trust in His character and what Jesus had done for me on the cross. God says about Himself; "For I *am* the Lord, I do not change" (Malachi 3:6a). If we know God's character, we will not be moved by the circumstances in our lives.

I have known times when I felt spiritually dry, and then I have also experienced how a great Bible teacher can open up the Word and stir my heart to want to read and study the Bible more. My prayer is that the Holy Spirit will stir up a hunger in you for God's Word and to know truth. I have learned that although we will not understand everything about God and the Bible, there is much we can understand about God. My desire is that this book will be a launching pad, drawing you into the Word of God, that it will draw you into a closer relationship with Jesus.

May your heart be stirred by what this God-man, Christ Jesus, did for you. May the cry of your heart be, *I want to know Jesus more.* He gave everything for you, and He is asking for your love in return. So often we have it backward in life; we might know the truth but the way we live portrays, "Jesus gave everything for me; I will work really hard for Him." Love comes first; otherwise we will grow weary in the task of trying to work for Him. When our works flow from a place of love and prayer they bear more fruit.

May the Holy Spirit reveal Jesus to you as you read this book. May Jesus become more real to you and speak to you in many different ways. May He give you the ears to hear what He is speaking to you and how He is working in your life. Above all, may He draw you into the love of this kind, wonderful, majestic Savior. "God so loved the world..." (John 3:16). Jesus is God's gift of love to the world. It is not a selfish love but a sacrificing love. It is a love that doesn't seek what He can gain but what He can give—giving the ultimate gift of His life for you on the cross.

Surrendering my life to Jesus was just the beginning of this journey. Through the years I heard His cry, "Will you love Me?" and I have grown to love Him more. Love makes every hardship, every injustice, every rejection, small compared to knowing and loving Him. That is the love that Paul discovered.

> "I count everything as loss compared to the possession of the priceless privilege (the overwhelming preciousness, the surpassing worth, and supreme advantage) of knowing Christ Jesus my Lord and of progressively becoming more deeply and intimately acquainted with Him [of perceiving and recognizing and understanding Him more fully and clearly]. …[For my determined purpose is] that I may know Him [that I may progressively become more deeply and intimately acquainted with Him, perceiving and recognizing and understanding the wonders of His Person more strongly and more clearly]" (Philippians 3:8, 10a AMP).

How to Use This Book for Group Discussion

This book can be read by itself or it can be used as small group material. When used for a small group, read the chapter that will be discussed ahead of time. If you have questions or thoughts about a section, mark it and talk about it in your group. Here are some ideas for how you can structure your group time and some basic guidelines you may want to set for your group to help keep things orderly.

Ideas for Group Time (One hour long)

- Welcome everyone and open with prayer.

- Use the first fifteen minutes to share questions or thoughts people had about the chapter. If someone has many questions and the leader feels it will take all the group time to answer them, then schedule a different time to talk about them unless you can put a time limit on the discussion and it will benefit the whole group.

- Use the next fifteen to twenty minutes for discussion questions. The questions are focused on digging deeper into Scripture and applying what each person is learning about God in their own lives. The questions don't have to be answered ahead of time; that can be done in the group.

- Use the remaining time for prayer and personal ministry. If the group is big enough and there are Christians who know how to pray for others, then divide the group in smaller groups of two or three people to pray. If the group is less than ten people, the person who wants to receive prayer can be seated in the middle while the others in the group pray for them. Often with this kind of prayer, the Holy Spirit will give different people impressions or pictures or prayers to pray that are very specific and helpful to the person being prayed for.

Set Some Guidelines for Discussion

- Don't get into any argumentative discussions. If questions come up that will take up a lot of group time, schedule a different time to discuss it with the person. Be sensitive to what the Holy Spirit wants to do. The purpose of the study is to grow personally. The purpose of the study is to get to know Jesus and talk about how He wants to meet us in our everyday life.

- Don't rush through the Scriptures; ask the Holy Spirit what He wants to speak to each of you as you go through the Scriptures and discuss them. The questions also have practical life application.

- The leader of the group should decide how to minister to those who need prayer.

Chapter 1: The Promise

"And I will put enmity between you and the woman, and between your seed and her Seed; He shall bruise your head, and you shall bruise His heel" (Genesis 3:15).

Once upon an eternal time, a splendid, majestic God created heavenly beings called angels. The angels worshiped Him and obeyed His orders (Psalms 103:20, 104:4). Eventually Lucifer and a group of the angels decided to rebel against God, and they were banished from His presence (Ezekiel 28:13-19). God inhabits eternity. He enjoys perfect love, peace, and communion with His Son, Jesus, and His Holy Spirit. They live in perfect harmony—three Persons, one God, never separated, always one in heart and mind. They are completely holy and pure, with no blemish or fault. Eternity is their home. God decided to create once again. He formed a place in Him where He would create a world and people created in His image. *Ones that could have relationship with Me! Is it possible? Would they willingly choose to love Me? Would they choose to obey Me? Would they learn to trust Me?* What if they choose wrong? In the world He was about to create there was a risk involved. Just as some of the angels chose not to serve God anymore, so His sons and daughters would have a choice, and they could choose not to serve Him. How painful would that be to His heart, to give them life and to see them turn against Him?

I am a parent, and I know how it blesses my heart to see my children happy and moving forward in life. I also know how it hurts my heart when I see a child struggle or make the wrong decisions. God knows my children and loves them even more than I do. "You saw me before I was born. Every day of my life was recorded in your book. Every moment was laid out before a single day had passed" (Psalm 139:16 NLT). If my heart aches when my children go through challenges, how much more does it hurt God's heart to see people whom He has created in His image struggle and suffer? God has a dream for you in His heart. He gives you a choice—will you follow your own way, or will you seek Him and walk in relationship with Him to find His best and most fruitful dream for your life?

Growing up, my mom and dad had dreams that their children would go to college. My dreams and prayers for my kids are that they will succeed in whatever they feel God has called them to do. I do at times wonder about God's plan for each of my children's lives. They were born with different strengths and gifts. Our daughter is very organized and precise. This gift helps her tremendously to be successful in her job. Our oldest son is good in math and science as well as music and sports. He could have gone in many different directions, but he chose engineering. The middle son is a prayer warrior and sensitive to the things of the Spirit. He is good in math and science too, and is seeking God about his future.

Our youngest son wanted to be a scientist or an inventor since he was four years old, so I thought Morgan would become an engineer, and he still might decide to do that. One Sunday morning during worship he had an encounter with God. He experienced this in a vision in his mind. Here he describes what happened:

> I was standing on a book, which I knew was my life story. I was walking on it, and I got to the middle where the binding is. There were pages missing, and on the other side there were blank pages. God showed me two sets of papers that were going to go in the space of the book that was missing. The first one was already written. The second one was blank. God told me He would let me write my own story and go to college, or I could let Him write my story. He basically said, *I will let you go to college, but it isn't My will for your life right now.*

This encounter dramatically changed Morgan's life. He decided to seek God about his future and went to Bible school for a year. This was a life-changing encounter that set his life on a different path. Morgan still has to ask and seek God daily for direction. Daily he has to make the right decisions and follow the Holy Spirit. The story of his life is being written as he walks in relationship with God—seeking, asking, listening, obeying, and loving God as he walks out life.

Through all of our lives a story is being written—individual stories, the stories of families, cities, and nations. Think of the leaders of countries: some leaders had to lead their people through times of war, while other leaders' lives tell sad stories of killing people and enriching themselves. If a leader makes wise decisions, then the people are blessed. I want my life story to read that I was a blessing to those who knew me.

The Bible tells the story of the history of mankind. Interwoven in this story we find the history of Jesus Christ, "His story," as He walked on earth as God and man according to the will of His heavenly Father. Given the choice to allow all of mankind to live separated from God forever or to give us the choice of redemption, Jesus chose and His choice was to do the will of His Father: "Father, if it is Your will, take this cup away from Me; nevertheless not My will, but Yours, be done" (Luke 22:42).

I wonder how long God thought about the decision to give man a free will. Do I create them to obey everything I say, with no ability to choose, or do I give them a choice and risk that they will kill each other, make war, and do terrible things? A relationship in which both people are blessed is so much more fulfilling. I have a wonderful friend who blesses me with her timely phone calls when she feels she should pray for me, and at other times I pray for her. We are a blessing to each other by praying together and having a friend to talk to and share with. There is much greater joy in a friendship when we give and receive than in being controlled in a relationship where we don't have a choice. God, knowing everything, knew that if He gave Adam and Eve free will, the time would come when they would make a wrong choice and a Savior would be needed to restore humanity back to Himself. He knew that even before He started to create the world (Revelation 13:8).

This is the story behind the story. An eternal Creator—God, who has all power and might, decided for a time period in eternity that people would walk out stories on earth and it would be called *history*. One picture can tell the story of a thousand words, and the Bible is full of such pictures. It tells stories of people who lived during history and God's dealings with them. We read about times when men or women turned their hearts toward God and it saved a nation (Jonah 1–4). We read about the results it had when people turned their backs to God and often it led to captivity. Moses addressed the Israelites and told them God was setting before them blessings or curses (Deuteronomy 30:1). Which one would they choose? Each one of us would think, *surely blessings*. Sometimes we make choices without knowing that they bring curses instead of blessings. In my Christian life I am walking through the process of learning what the Bible says, following the Holy Spirit, and learning to make decisions that will bring spiritual life to me, my family, and my walk with God.

Let us go back to the beginning. The Bible starts off with God creating. "In the beginning God created the heavens and the earth" (Genesis 1:1). Several times in Genesis 1 we read how God spoke and it happened, again and again, and through His spoken Word the heavens, the earth, and everything upon it were created. Creation reveals the involvement of a triune God. God spoke; we find the Holy Spirit brooding over the earth (Genesis 1:2). Jesus was present too. Jesus is the Word. We learn this in John. "In the beginning was the Word, and the Word was with God, and the Word was God. He was in the beginning with God. All things were made through Him, and without Him nothing was made that was made" (John 1:1-3).

I can't even wrap my mind around this Scripture. Everything was made through Jesus. Some Scriptures you just have to believe; they are just too big for my small mind. As I continued to read through John 1, I thought verse 10 was one of the saddest verses in the Bible. It says that even though Jesus created the world, the world didn't recognize Him when He walked the earth (John 1:10). When John the Baptist baptized Jesus, we see the Trinity. Jesus was in the water, being baptized. God the Father spoke from heaven, saying, "This is My beloved Son, in whom I am well pleased" (Matthew 3:17). The Holy Spirit descended upon Jesus, empowering Him for ministry. Even though this book will focus on who Jesus is, I don't want us to forget that God reveals Himself to us in the Bible as one God, three Persons.

God looked at His creation and said it was very good. He placed Adam and Eve in a beautiful, perfect garden called Eden. Their relationship with God reminds me of the relationship between a parent and a young child. A few years ago I visited friends. I was very impressed to see how their kids asked their mom if they could have candy and then ate only the amount they were allowed to eat. I could see how they honored and obeyed their mother. The thought of eating more than what their mother said had not yet entered their minds.

That was how Adam and Eve were; they were trusting, obeying God with a childlike innocence. Adam and Eve received one instruction from God, one rule to obey. God told them not to eat from the Tree of the Knowledge of Good and Evil; if they did, they would die. All went well until the Serpent came and sowed doubt in Eve's mind. He asked her if God said that they should not eat any of the fruit of the garden. The Serpent was setting a trap for Eve. In her naïveté she didn't know or see it. The conversation led her to taste the fruit of the forbidden tree and she gave Adam some too (Genesis 3:1-6).

Within three chapters of the beginning of the Bible, we read how one decision ruined that perfect garden for Adam and Eve. The Tree of Life was in the middle of the garden too. If Adam and Eve ate from this tree, they would receive everlasting life. God could not allow Adam and Eve to eat from this tree and stay in the state of being separated from Him because of their disobedience. He had to banish them from the garden they called home. God placed an angel at the entrance of the garden to guard it. Adam and Eve could not return, and they lost the intimate fellowship they had with God in the garden. There was no way back; they needed to be redeemed by the One who would step into their place, the only One who could meet the requirements of God.

Disobeying God had consequences. The snake found itself cursed by God to sail on his belly. Childbirth would be painful for Eve, and God placed a curse on the ground that it would take hard work and sweat for Adam to make a living. In the midst of all the bad news, God gave them hope. He gave them a promise—that one of Eve's offspring would trample on the Serpent's head (Genesis 3:14-19). In the garden, Satan came as a snake. He is mankind's enemy, and the promise was given to Adam and Eve that one of their offspring would defeat Satan. God already revealed His plan for redemption here at the beginning of the Bible—that somewhere down the generational line a Rescuer, a Savior would be born to redeem mankind. God's plan always includes restoration and second chances.

As I read through Genesis, I saw how many times the word *covenant* was used. In Bible times, a covenant was an agreement between people or an agreement between God and people (Genesis 9:11-13; 21:27). In modern times, we can compare it to a business or marriage contract. The first time we read about a covenant is with Noah. Noah was a righteous man. He walked in close fellowship with God. He was the only blameless man God could find at that time (Genesis 6:9). God told Noah to build an ark, and then fill it with animals. It rained for forty days and forty nights and the earth flooded. Only Noah, his family, and the animals in the ark survived the flood. The first thing Noah did when he came out of the ark was to build an altar and offer a sacrifice to God. God was pleased with his offering and He made a covenant with Noah. He gave the rainbow as a sign of the covenant and God promised not to destroy the earth again with a flood. "When I see the rainbow in the clouds, I will remember the eternal covenant between God and every living creature on earth" (Genesis 9:16 NLT). God made the promise, and nothing anyone can do will change God's promise. This covenant is not conditional on what people do or don't do. Some covenants have conditions attached to their promises.

In Genesis 17 we read about the covenant God made with Abraham; the sign of this covenant was circumcision. Abraham's father worshiped other gods (Joshua 24:2). Abraham was searching for the one true living God, and when he found God he left his homeland and followed God. We see that Abraham's faith journey was a process. Abraham didn't do everything right from the beginning of his faith walk. When Abraham's journey took him to Egypt, he feared that he would be killed and his beautiful wife taken from him. He asked Sarah to tell the people that she was his sister. God intervened and showed the king in a dream not to touch Sarah. When God's promise to give them a son was slow to come into fulfillment, Sarah gave Abraham her servant to have a son. This was not God's best plan, and it caused problems in the family.

Finally when Abraham was a hundred years old, Isaac was born. Abraham's faith grew over the years and became stronger. God tested Abraham and asked him to sacrifice his son, Isaac. Abraham set out on this journey to Mount Moriah to offer his son. This time Abraham was obedient. He tied Isaac to the altar and just before he was going to kill Isaac, he heard the angel of the Lord telling him not to hurt Isaac. Now God knew that Abraham feared Him. Abraham looked and there was a ram in the bush. God had provided a ram for a sacrifice (Genesis 22:1-18). Abraham's faith grew from wavering at times when he thought his life was in danger to trusting God to such an extent that he was willing to be obedient to God and give up his son, Isaac, when God asked him to.

On his journey, Abraham met Abimelech who wanted to make a covenant with him. Abimelech saw that God was with Abraham, helping him in everything he did (Genesis 21:22). "Now Abraham was old, well advanced in age; and the Lord had blessed Abraham in all things" (Genesis 24:1). One day in heaven I would like to sit and listen to the people whose lives we read about in the Bible and hear them tell their life stories. I would like to hear what Abraham's secret was, why God blessed him in everything he did. We read about Isaac, Abraham's son, that the Lord blessed him too. He harvested a hundred times more than what he planted and he became very prosperous (Genesis 26:12). God prospered them to be a blessing to those around them. Their lives were a living testimony of the goodness of God. One thing I can see from this is that obedience to God will bring a blessing.

One day as I was driving to the store, I was thinking about my children and their desire to follow God. Finances have been a challenge, but they managed to go to Bible school and they are pursuing God. I realized that some people are called into full-time ministry and others are called into the marketplace. That morning my eyes were opened to see how God wants to provide for those who are called into missions or ministry through those who work in the marketplace. God's plan is to advance His kingdom. He gives us the finances to steward it carefully. The world we live in will pass away. I will never forget what my mom told me when my grandma passed away. She went to the nursing home to pick up my grandma's stuff; it all fit in one small suitcase. She said we accumulate stuff, not realizing we enter this world with nothing and we leave this earth with nothing. We are not able to take any of our earthly possessions with us. Even the money we earn in a job is God's provision for us, and therefore we need to be good stewards with what He gives us.

Now let's follow Abraham's descendants—Isaac, Jacob, and Joseph. Joseph was Jacob's favorite son. His brothers were jealous of him. When he took food to them in the field, they schemed to kill him. Reuben tried to save Joseph and suggested that they throw him in an empty well. Ishmaelite slave traders came by, and Joseph's brothers sold him to them before Reuben could return to rescue him. The slave traders sold Joseph in Egypt to Potiphar, a member of Pharaoh's staff. God blessed Joseph, and he was put in charge of the administration of Potiphar's house. Even though Joseph lived in a foreign country, he still followed the ways he was raised in. Potiphar's wife became angry when Joseph refused her attentions, and he was thrown into prison. Even in prison God's favor was upon Joseph, "But the Lord was with Joseph there, too, and was kind to him by granting him favor with the chief jailer. In fact, the jailer soon handed over the entire prison administration to Joseph, so that all the other prisoners were responsible to him. The chief jailer had no more worries after that, for Joseph took care of everything, and the Lord was with him so that everything ran smoothly and well" (Genesis 39:21-23 TLB).

This is a picture of God's favor and blessing. Everywhere Joseph went, he prospered. God was with him and helped him (Genesis 39–41). God can work through us just like Joseph in the areas of politics, engineering, business, every area of life. Our faith in Jesus can work in our everyday life if we allow Him in. I see how He gives my husband ideas for his job. God uses our natural gifts and talents and the training we receive, but top that off with supernatural wisdom and we see supernatural results. We can have no better business partner and help in our work than allowing God to move in, and through, us, even in our everyday situations.

I have given just a few examples of covenant. Abraham turned to God and God made promises to him that his descendants would become nations (Genesis 17:6-8). We follow God's dealings with Abraham and his descendants through the Old Testament. They are sometimes called God's covenant people. God made promises to them, and when they obeyed God, they lived under the covenant blessings of God. "Then [Jacob] blessed Joseph and said, God [Himself], before Whom my fathers Abraham and Isaac lived and walked habitually, God [Himself], Who has [been my Shepherd and has led and] fed me from the time I came into being until this day" (Genesis 48:15 AMP). Hebrews 11 is the Bible's "hall of fame"—the heroes of the faith. There is one thing that all these heroes have in common, and that is that they trusted God. They had faith in God, and because of their faith God received them; He blessed them and worked through them to be a blessing to others. We can read about the lives of others who had a relationship with God and learn from their lives. We can follow their successes and learn from their failures.

The Old Testament contains God's dealings with His people before the birth of Jesus, and the New Testament is about the birth, life, death, and resurrection of Jesus and the early church. God desires to have a relationship with people. It is a covenant relationship, which is a deep, wholehearted commitment in which a person surrenders their whole life to God. This is what He is drawing you into. When you do not know Him, it might not be as easy to surrender. When you get to know Jesus and how much He loves you, His love draws you in to willing surrender. Draw us with Your love, Jesus!

Discovering Jesus

Discussion Questions: The Promise

1. Describe what a good relationship between loving parents and a child looks like, and the ideals and expectations a parent should have for a child.

2. Do you see God as such a parent? Is your view of God different from how you view a good parent? Do you feel God is a good parent? (See Romans 8:28 and Jeremiah 29:11.)

3. Take the open book encounter my son had as a personal message to you and write down your thoughts. Would you have to change things in your life if you allowed God to write the story of your life? Discuss.

4. Your relationship with God:

a) Describe your view of a relationship with God.

b) Share ideas of what a person can do to grow in their relationship with God.

5. Ponder the Word: Read the two Scriptures below. Take some time and focus on a word or phrase in the Scripture and write down thoughts about it. If there is time, give an opportunity to share about it.

"And Enoch walked [in habitual fellowship] with God; and he was not, for God took him [home with Him]" (Genesis 5:24 AMP).

"Then [Jacob] blessed Joseph and said, God [Himself], before Whom my fathers Abraham and Isaac lived and walked habitually, God [Himself], Who has [been my Shepherd and has led and] fed me from the time I came into being until this day" (Genesis 48:15 AMP).

_____
_____
_____
_____
_____
_____
_____
_____
_____

Chapter 2: Jesus, Gift from Heaven to Earth

> "In the beginning the Word already existed. The Word was with God, and the Word was God. ...So the Word became human and made his home among us" (John 1:1,14 NLT).

When I open a children's Bible I see pictures of Jesus. I see Him lying in a manger, growing up, and starting His ministry. Eventually I read about His death on the cross and resurrection. Seeing these pictures formed the impression in my mind that the first time Jesus came into existence was when He was born as a baby. That assumption is not true. Jesus existed with God as the second Person of the Trinity in eternity. Jesus, the Son of the living God, is described as the Lamb slain before the foundation of the earth (Revelation 13:8). He existed outside of time with God. In the book of John, we meet Jesus as the Word, who was in the beginning with God (John 1:1-3). Everything seen and unseen were made through Him and for Him (Colossians 1:16-17). We read that Jesus is the One "maintaining and guiding and propelling the universe by His mighty word of power" (Hebrews 1:3b AMP). These Scriptures are too big for my mind to comprehend. Believing in a God who is much bigger than my mind can comprehend and understand is comforting to me, because I can trust my life into His hands and know that He knows the bigger picture and has my best interests in mind. If He holds the world together, then surely He knows what is best for my life and He can hold my life together. Jesus, "existed before all things, and in Him all things consist (cohere, are held together)" (Colossians 1:17 AMP).

What did Jesus look like? In Colossians we learn that Jesus "is the exact likeness of the unseen God [the visible representation of the invisible]" (Colossians 1:15 AMP). When we think about Jesus as the image or likeness of God, we tend to think of His physical appearance. Jesus, being Jewish, most likely looked like someone from Jewish descent. The Message Bible describes Jesus coming to earth this way: "The Word became flesh and blood, and moved into the neighborhood" (John 1:14 MSG). It continues, "This one-of-a-kind God-Expression, who exists at the very heart of the Father, has made him plain as day" (John 1:18 MSG).

Isaiah prophesied that there would be nothing in Jesus' appearance that would attract people to Him. Jesus lived in a body, but He operated from a different place. He connected with God in His spirit and walked in fellowship and obedience with His Father. He didn't rely on His human strength, but operated in the wisdom and power of the Holy Spirit. He listened to and obeyed what God showed Him to do. As He walked on earth, He healed people, and shared parables with them, He revealed to them who God was. He walked the earth fully God but also fully man— Son of God and Son of man (John 1:34; Matthew 9:6; Matthew 12:8). He didn't exalt Himself. He humbled Himself and modeled a picture of living in relationship and obedience to God (John 5:19; Philippians 2:7-11).

Let us start this journey with Zechariah. He was a priest in the temple in Jerusalem. Zechariah was minding his own business, doing his priestly duties, and suddenly the angel Gabriel showed up. Naturally he was shaken, full of fear, and wondered, *What is going on?* This was how most people in the Bible reacted when an angel showed up. The angel told him not to be afraid. He gave him the news—that God heard his prayers and his wife, Elizabeth, would become pregnant. They would have a baby and should name him John. The angel also told him about the destiny of the child. He would be filled with the Holy Spirit even before his birth, and he would turn many back to God (Luke 1:15-16). John the Baptist was the one who was prophesied of in Isaiah who would prepare the way before the Lord (Jesus) (Isaiah 40:3). John lived in the desert where he devoted his life to God. His message touched many: "Repent, for the kingdom of heaven is at hand!" (Matthew 3:2). Many turned and were baptized by John and His disciples.

This was a time when the Jewish people were expectantly awaiting the arrival of a Savior. The Roman Empire ruled the civilized world. They desired to be rescued from Roman rule. God had more in mind than rescuing them from an earthly government. Eve received the promise of the One who would crush the Serpent's head. The prophets prophesied of a promised Messiah. They said that His mother would conceive Him as a virgin, and He would be called Immanuel, which means "God is with us" (Isaiah 7:14 NLT). Isaiah prophesied about Him, "For unto us a Child is born, unto us a Son is given; and the government will be upon His shoulder. And His name will be called Wonderful, Counselor, Mighty God, Everlasting Father, Prince of Peace" (Isaiah 9:6). Isaiah's prophecy also revealed that the Savior would be born from the generational line of Jesse, who was David's father (Matthew 1:6). The Holy Spirit would rest upon Him, and He would walk in respect, reverence, and obedience to God (Isaiah 11:1-3). They were waiting for a God-man to arrive—the Messiah, the Son of the living God!

Think about it this way. I have had the experience of meeting a lady over the phone, and then eventually I met her in person. When I finally met her I was surprised because she looked different than I had imagined. This is the same with Jesus. The Israelites learned about God through the Law and the life stories of their forefathers, Abraham, Isaac, and Jacob. They had a picture in their mind of who the Messiah would be, but when He came they didn't recognize Him (John 1:11).

We read about many supernatural events happening around the birth of Jesus. Heaven and earth worked together; angels showed up several times delivering messages. After the message given to Zechariah, God's plan continued with a young Jewish girl named Mary who was engaged to a young man, Joseph. God interrupted her life suddenly. An angel showed up. "'Don't be afraid, Mary,' the angel told her, 'for you have found favor with God! You will conceive and give birth to a son, and you will name him Jesus'" (Luke 1:30-31 NLT). The angel told her the baby would be the Son of God and His kingdom would never end. Mary asked the angel how this was possible. He told her the Holy Spirit would overshadow her and she would become pregnant. Mary responded and said, "Let it be to me according to your word" (Luke 1:38). She didn't hesitate; she didn't give an excuse. This event would interrupt her plans and possibly end her engagement to Joseph, but she didn't hesitate. She answered *yes* to what God asked of her.

Her fiancé, Joseph, decided to break the engagement quietly. God intervened and sent an angel to visit Joseph in a dream. The angel told Joseph that the child was conceived by the Holy Spirit. He should be named Jesus, which means Savior, because He would save His people from their sins (Matthew 1:20-21). Joseph changed his mind and married Mary. During that time, Caesar Augustus decided to take a census. Everyone had to register for the census in their hometown. Joseph journeyed with a very pregnant Mary from Galilee to Bethlehem. There was no room in the inn, but the innkeeper told them they could sleep in the stable. When Jesus was born, there was no room for Him; He is still asking if we will make room for Him in our hearts. Mary gave birth in the humble surroundings of a stable (Luke 2:7). When you surrender your life to Jesus, it is an act of humility, laying down your plans and submitting to Jesus'. Although most of the people weren't aware of what was happening, heaven was excited!

Can you imagine God's excitement? *My Son, He is born! That baby, He is my Son! Who can I tell; who will listen?* There were shepherds out in the field; they received the surprise visit. The Passion Translation describes this angelic visit beautifully: "Don't be afraid. For I have come to bring you good news, the most joyous news the world has ever heard! And it is for everyone, everywhere! For today in Bethlehem a Rescuer was born for you! He is the Anointed Messiah, the LORD JEHOVAH!" (Luke 2:10-11 TPT). The angels told them the Savior was lying in a manger, and He was wrapped in cloth. A host of angels came and sang praises to God.

What a surprise! These shepherds thought it was just going to be another boring night of watching sheep. *Angels! A Savior! We have to go and see if we can find Him!* They found Him in the stable in Bethlehem and told many about what happened (Luke 2:16-17). This was a major moment in world history. Our time is still divided into BC ("Before Christ") and AD (*Anno Domini*—Latin for "the year of our Lord" referring to each year after He was born). God didn't tell the kings of the earth; He told shepherds who were watching sheep in the field. Someone else knew too. Wise men from the East followed a star to Bethlehem. They went to King Herod and asked him about the child. Herod wasn't happy that a child was born who could possibly become king. He told the wise men to let him know if they found this child. The wise men followed the star and found Jesus. They worshiped Him and gave Him gifts—gold, frankincense, and myrrh. God warned them through a dream not to go to back to Herod, and they took a different road home (Matthew 2:1-12).

God prepared others too who were awaiting the birth of Jesus. Simeon was a righteous man, and the Holy Spirit revealed to him that he would not die before he saw the Messiah. According to the Law, the firstborn child had to be dedicated to God. The parents brought an offering—either two turtledoves or pigeons. Joseph and Mary took Jesus to the temple. The Holy Spirit led Simeon to the temple at the same time, and he prophesied over Jesus, "He is a light to reveal God to the nations, and he is the glory of your people Israel!" (Luke 2:32 NLT). Anna, a prophetess who stayed at the temple day and night, came in as Simeon blessed Jesus. She began to praise God and talked to everyone about Jesus (Luke 2:25-38). Reading about the shepherds, the wise men, Simeon, and Anna stirs one's heart to be one of those in tune with heaven—one who God can share His secrets with. He does speak to those who want to listen.

Jesus was not safe. Herod wanted to kill the child, the One who was said to be the King of the Jews. An angel appeared to Joseph in a dream and warned him that Herod wanted to kill Jesus. He told Joseph to take Mary and Jesus and flee to Egypt (Matthew 2:13). They escaped from Herod's decree, which called for all the children younger than two years old to be killed in Bethlehem and the surrounding district (Matthew 2:16). Later when Herod died, God gave Joseph directions in a dream to go back to their home country. They settled in Nazareth (Matthew 2:19-23).

We don't read much about the childhood years of Jesus. We read that as He grew up, He was filled with wisdom and that the grace of God was upon His life (Luke 2:40). One account is written in the Bible. Joseph and Mary went to Jerusalem every year for the Passover Feast. When Jesus was twelve years old, they went as usual. On the way back, Joseph and Mary realized Jesus was not amongst them, and they turned back to go and look for Jesus. They found him in the temple, sitting with the religious teachers, listening to them and asking questions. Everybody was surprised by His understanding. His mother and father were upset that they hadn't been able to find him. Look at the response of Jesus at age twelve: "'But why did you need to search?' he asked. 'Didn't you know that I must be in my Father's house?' ...Then he returned to Nazareth with them and was obedient to them" (Luke 2:49, 51a NLT). At twelve years old, Jesus already had the revelation that God was His Father. His parents didn't understand what He meant, but we read that, "Mary kept all these things and pondered them in her heart" (Luke 2:19).

Jesus was born into a Jewish culture. He had Jewish parents. He learned and lived the Jewish customs of those times. In Bible times children learned differently than they learn today. A son learned how to build a house by observing how his dad measured and calculated when he was building. The children learned about money by going to the market with their mother and observing how she counted money to buy fruit, vegetables, or cloth. The girls learned to cook by helping their mother. In the evenings the family gathered and the stories of history were told. Learning focused more on gaining wisdom for living.[3]

Jewish children started to memorize the Torah (the first five books of the Bible, also called the Pentateuch) and other Old Testament Scriptures by age five or six. They started to learn the Oral Torah (the rabbis' traditional interpretations of the Torah passed on orally) after age ten. Boys started to learn a trade by age thirteen, and only the most talented continued to study and would become disciples of a rabbi.[4]

This is the culture that Jesus grew up in. The incident when Jesus stayed behind in the temple at age twelve reveals to us that He had an above average interest in the Scriptures. "All who heard him were

---

3. Ann Spangler and Lois Tverberg, *Sitting at the Feet of Rabbi Jesus: How the Jewishness of Jesus Can Transform Your Faith* (Grand Rapids, MI: Zondervan, 2009), 53. Used by Permission of Zondervan. www.Zondervan.com.
4. Ibid., 24-25.

amazed at his understanding and his answers" (Luke 2:47 NLT). He didn't have the opportunity to learn from the best rabbis of His time. Just like most boys of His time, He learned the trade of His father—that of a carpenter (Mark 6:3).

For thirty years Jesus lived a normal life, and then something significant happened. His cousin, John the Baptist, was preaching in the wilderness. He was preparing the people for the coming of the Messiah. The people had an expectation that the Messiah would come, and they wondered if John the Baptist was the Messiah (Luke 3:15). One day John was preaching, and Jesus showed up and asked to be baptized. John (a cousin of Jesus) recognized Jesus and told Him that he was the one who should be baptized by Jesus. Jesus insisted that this was how God wanted it to be. John baptized Jesus. The heavens opened as Jesus came up out the water, "and He saw the Spirit of God descending like a dove and alighting upon Him. And suddenly a voice came from heaven, saying, 'This is My beloved Son, in whom I am well pleased'" (Matthew 3:16b-17). This was before Jesus started His ministry; this was before Jesus did any miracles. God loves Jesus because He is God's Son. Later Jesus said that in the same way the Father loves Him, He loves us (John 15:9).

When my children were little, I was full of zeal for God. I wanted to do God's will and be involved with His work in some way. My life was so busy raising four little ones that I didn't have much time to do a whole lot more. One morning I read this Scripture in Proverbs 3:27: "Do not withhold good from those to whom it is due, when it is in the power of your hand to do so." I realized sometimes God sends someone across my path that needs help, and it is in my ability to help. I began to recognize the day-to-day opportunities God placed before me. It is helpful to know which age group you minister to best—children, adults, or the elderly. It is encouraging to see how many families are stirred to foster or adopt children. Are you an encourager? For many years when my children were young God had me write encouraging notes to people. I was obedient to do that when He prompted me. Often the people told me how blessed they were and how timely the word was, and it helped me to learn to recognize God's voice when I was obedient to those small promptings and did something seemingly so small as encouraging someone.

Let's pick up the story again. Jesus was baptized by John the Baptist and the Holy Spirit came upon Him. Think of all the things God could have said to His Son in this situation. God didn't say, *You are My Son who is going to do many miracles,* or *Son, don't fail Me.* God affirmed Jesus and spoke of His love for His Son when He released Him into the purpose that He came to earth to accomplish. "And a voice from heaven said, 'This is my dearly loved Son, who brings me great joy'" (Matthew 3:17 NLT). No matter what we do for God, He is interested in having a relationship with us, and He is not just interested in the work we can do for Him. In most religions, people try to please their god. They pray at particular times of the day, do good deeds, live a certain way, always doing, doing, doing something to try and receive the approval of their god. That is how the Pharisees and Sadducees lived too. They obeyed a lot of rules to please God. It is so much more pleasurable to obey God because He loves us and we love Him than to just work hard for Him. "You did not choose Me, but I chose you" (John 15:16a).

Jesus received an empowering for ministry at His baptism. What a wonderful experience. Jesus was baptized and filled with the Holy Spirit, and then instead of doing His first miracle, He was led into the desert by the Holy Spirit for forty days to fast and be tempted by the Devil. "Then Jesus, full of and controlled by the Holy Spirit, returned from the Jordan and was led in [by] the [Holy] Spirit. For (during) forty days in the wilderness (desert), where He was tempted (tried, tested exceedingly) by the devil" (Luke 4:1-2 AMP).

We read that Jesus was hungry. Satan tempted Him to turn the stones into bread. Jesus answered from Scripture, "It is written, 'Man shall not live by bread alone, but by every word of God'" (Luke 4:4). Jesus responded with Scripture to every temptation Satan brought to Him. Satan works through deception. Satan even tried to trick Jesus by using Scripture improperly. But understanding Scripture digs a deep foundation within us. If we know the truth he cannot deceive us.

Memorizing the Torah (the first five books of the Bible) and other books of the Bible was an important foundation for Jesus to know the truth.

The first thirty years of Jesus' life, God prepared Him to be able to walk under the tremendous pressure of ministry—teaching, preaching, healing, and doing miracles. Jesus was secure in His relationship with His Father. He obeyed God rather than pleased men (John 15:9).

Discussion Questions: Jesus, Gift from Heaven

1. Share briefly the picture you had of Jesus before you started to read this book. Read Colossians 1:16-17 and Hebrews 1:1-3. Do these Scriptures change the picture of Jesus that you just described? What is the difference?

2. Jesus was the living picture of God the Father on earth. From the knowledge that you have of Jesus and the Bible, give a short description of what that picture looks like to you.

3. God sent John the Baptist to prepare the way before Jesus. God sees the bigger picture. Look at your life and write down some of the things that you can see God has orchestrated for you to become the person you are. Share some of your thoughts around this.

4. Think of the areas that God has gifted you in and how you could use that to help people. Write down a few thoughts. Discuss some of the ideas.

5. God said of Jesus, "This is My beloved Son" (Matthew 3:17). Write a letter from God to yourself. Write what you feel in your heart; how does He see you? (This can be done as homework if there is not enough time during the group.)

_____
_____
_____

6. Ponder the Word: We see how God felt about Jesus when Jesus was baptized (Matthew 3:16-17). Take time to ponder John 15:9 and John 15:15. Write down your thoughts about these Scriptures. Share if there is time.

_____
_____
_____
_____
_____

Chapter 3: Jesus Starts His Ministry

"For God so loved the world that He gave His only begotten Son, that whoever believes in Him should not perish but have everlasting life" (John 3:16).

How did John the Baptist know Jesus was the Messiah? John said that God told him that the one on whom he saw the Holy Spirit descend would be the One who would baptize people with the Holy Spirit (John 1:33). When John baptized Jesus, the heavens opened and the Holy Spirit came upon Jesus and confirmed that Jesus was indeed the Savior. The next day when Jesus walked by, John said, "Behold! The Lamb of God who takes away the sin of the world!" (John 1:29). He was referring to Exodus 12:3 where God gave Moses and Aaron instructions to kill a lamb and put the blood on the sides of the door so that they would be protected when all the firstborn of Egypt were killed. He also referred to Isaiah 53:7, which is a prophecy of the Messiah—He would be like a lamb led to be slaughtered. The Israelites had celebrated the Passover, a commemoration of when God delivered them out of Egypt, sending ten plagues upon the Egyptians, ever since they left Egypt nearly 2,000 years ago. Their reference to a lamb is the Passover lamb, a picture of the coming Messiah, the Savior.

When Jesus lived on earth, rabbis (religious teachers) had disciples who lived with them and followed them everywhere they went. These disciples learned from the rabbis. They did not only learn the interpretation of the Scriptures, they learned to imitate the rabbis' lives.[5] When Jesus came out of the desert, He called men to be His disciples. Two of John's disciples followed Jesus. Next Jesus told Philip, "Come, follow me" (John 1:43 NLT). Jesus called twelve disciples whom He taught for three years while He walked and ministered on the earth.

Jesus is calling you too—"Come, follow Me." He doesn't just desire that a person would receive Him and then go their own way. He desires the commitment of a disciple. A disciple lived with a rabbi, observed how he lived life, and followed his example. "An Eastern view of discipleship seems far more in keeping with the gospel. The Eastern view encompasses the understanding that Jesus died for our sins and that belonging to Him involves repenting and receiving Him as Lord. But it also recognizes that Jesus lived transparently in front of His disciples in order to teach them how to live. They, in turn, were to live transparently before others, humbly teaching them the way of Christ. This approach involves not just information, but transformation." [6]

Today we don't have Jesus physically living with us, but we read about Him in the Bible and learn from the Bible how to live. When we surrender our lives to Jesus, His Holy Spirit comes and lives on the inside of us, to lead and guide us daily (John 14:16-17). You can walk with Him daily and read the Bible, and the Holy Spirit will teach you. We commit to involve Jesus in every area of our lives. When you get used to living life that way, you will not want to live any other way. It is worth a wholehearted commitment to see Jesus answer prayer and move in our everyday life. He doesn't always move the way we think He will, but He always brings us through every situation. One day I spoke with my son when he was going through a difficult time. He didn't enjoy the summer job he had. I told him, "This is not the end of the story. Jesus doesn't just leave us in a difficult situation and not help us. This situation won't last forever. We might experience difficulty, but as we present it to God in prayer and ask His help, He opens the way to help

---

5. Ann Spangler and Lois Tverberg, *Sitting at the Feet of Rabbi Jesus: How the Jewishness of Jesus Can Transform Your Faith* (Grand Rapids, MI: Zondervan, 2009), 55. Used by Permission of Zondervan. www.Zondervan.com.
6. Ibid., 64.

us through." By the end of the summer, my son could look back and saw that his life and interactions did have an impact on those he worked with as well as himself.

The Pharisees and the Sadducees were the two main Jewish religious groups at that time (see Matthew 3:7). The Pharisees separated themselves from anything that was not Jewish and followed the Old Testament rules and traditions that had been handed down through the centuries. The Sadducees followed the Pentateuch (the first five books of the Bible), and they were mostly descendants of the Levites and the priests, while the Pharisees came from all classes of people. Both groups were against Jesus.

Jesus was addressed as "Rabbi" (see Matthew 26:25; Mark 9:5) or "Rabboni" (see Mark 10:51; John 20:16), which was a title used by the Jews to address their teachers. It is a title of respect similar to the way we address a physician as *doctor*, or the leader of a church as *pastor, minister,* or *reverend*.

Jesus was born in a time when Israel was struggling under the weight of Roman taxes and oppression. There was a spiritual hunger for truth and a desire to return to God's ways. It was a time when the Jewish people longed for the Messiah to appear.[7] Jesus came for much more than to free them from Roman oppression. He came to offer them the gift of eternal life.

In John 3 we read about a Jewish religious leader who visited Jesus one evening. He was hungry to know truth and told Jesus he believed that God was with Him. Jesus gave an astonishing answer to Nicodemus; He told him, "Most assuredly, I say to you, unless one is born again, he cannot see the kingdom of God" (John 3:3). Nicodemus didn't understand. Jesus explained that a person should be born from water and the Spirit to enter the kingdom of God (John 3:5-6). We see here a fleshly birth—we are born from our mother's womb when the water breaks. Then we see a spiritual birth, when the Holy Spirit works

---

7. Ann Spangler and Lois Tverberg, *Sitting at the Feet of Rabbi Jesus: How the Jewishness of Jesus Can Transform Your Faith* (Grand Rapids, MI: Zondervan, 2009), 24. Used by Permission of Zondervan. www.Zondervan.com.

in our hearts and draws us to surrender our lives to Jesus. "Humans can reproduce only human life, but the Holy Spirit gives birth to spiritual life" (John 3:6 NLT).

The stirring in your heart to follow Jesus, the desire to get to know Him, is a Holy Spirit work. Jesus gave the example of the wind. Just as we hear the wind blowing but can't tell where it comes from or where it is going, we can't explain how God's Spirit works in human hearts to draw them to Jesus. Jesus was revealing a kingdom secret to Nicodemus. He continued to tell him that God sent His only Son so that people would not perish but could receive everlasting life. Think for a minute how Nicodemus must have felt. Here he was—a Pharisee, a religious scholar, and Jesus talked to him about being born again. I think if I were Nicodemus I would have felt astonished, blown away by Jesus' teaching. This is so different than the way Nicodemus was taught. Nicodemus thought salvation came through keeping God's laws. Jesus showed him a different way: "For God did not send His Son into the world to condemn the world, but that the world through Him might be saved" (John 3:17).

Jesus was showing Nicodemus a new way of salvation—salvation through believing in Jesus, the Son of God. He said God the Father put everything in Jesus' hands and gave Jesus to the world so that no one should die and be separated from God. Everyone who believes in Jesus will receive eternal life (John 3:35-36). Jesus gave Nicodemus much to think about. He was a Pharisee, a teacher of the Law, and he needed Jesus to receive eternal life?

In May of 1999 we moved from our home country, South Africa, to the USA. We weren't able to go back for a visit until 2013. When we finally visited, it was a wonderful time of catching up with our family. Night after night we sat around the dinner table as we visited our family. They were tremendous hosts. We enjoyed wonderful food and company. We felt loved and welcomed. We had a rich, blessed time as we experienced great hospitality. It was refreshing to take a break out of our busy lives and slow down and catch up with family. Spending the time around the dinner table made me realize what a blessing such a time can be.

Jesus was born into a culture where hospitality was a natural part of life. People walked where they wanted to go. It was a very hot climate. Offering a drink of water to someone was not only hospitable, but could save a life.[8] "You can approach any of the residents in this ancient land for food, water, and shelter and they would provide it."[9] They visited with people around meals. It was a time of talking, visiting, and discussion. Weddings were important times of celebration and lasted seven days. Many were invited and the invitation could even include the whole town. It would be an insult not to accept an invitation to a wedding. Great care was taken with the preparations and to run out of wine would be an embarrassment to the family. In this kind of culture, Jesus and His family went to a wedding. The wine ran out before the wedding was over. Mary asked Jesus to help. He didn't respond when she asked Him, but waited until He heard from His Father. Then He asked the servants to fill the stone jars with water. He told them to take it to the person in charge of the wedding. When the man tasted it, he asked the bridegroom why they reserved the best wine for last; usually the host served the best wine first (John 2:1-12). This was Jesus' first miracle, "This beginning of signs Jesus did in Cana of Galilee, and manifested His glory; and His disciples believed in Him" (John 2:11). Jesus "manifested His glory" or "revealed His glory" (NLT); this was the first time the supernatural power of the Holy Spirit manifested through Jesus and a miracle was performed.

We follow Jesus to the temple in Jerusalem during the Passover celebration, and what do we see? He made a whip and chased out the merchants selling cattle, sheep, and doves for sacrifices. People had turned His Father's house, the temple, into a marketplace. The disciples remembered the prophecy, "Passion for God's house will consume me" (John 2:17 NLT, see Ps. 69:9). The Jewish leaders asked Jesus for a sign to prove that God gave Him the authority to do this. Jesus said, "Destroy

---
8. Ann Spangler and Lois Tverberg, *Sitting at the Feet of Rabbi Jesus: How the Jewishness of Jesus Can Transform Your Faith* (Grand Rapids, MI: Zondervan, 2009), 131-132. Used by Permission of Zondervan. www.Zondervan.com.
9. Ibid., 130.

this temple, and in three days I will raise it up" (John 2:19 NLT). The Jewish leaders didn't understand what Jesus was saying; they thought He was referring to the physical building. Jesus was referring to His body dying on the cross, and after three days, He would rise from the dead. The disciples remembered this after Jesus rose from the dead, and they believed Jesus and the Scriptures (John 2:13-22).

The feasts that the Israelites celebrated all had some picture of Jesus in them. In the Feast of Tabernacles we see a ritual with water. "The first was the ritual of the pouring of water. This took place on the last day of the Feast of Tabernacles. The day was called in Hebrew *Hoshanah Rabbah*, which means the 'Day of the Great Hosannah.' This Hebrew phrase translates into English as 'save now' or 'deliver us!' The Day of the Great Hosanna was the day when the Jews would pray for rain and God's salvation through the Messiah."[10]

This occurred at the beginning of the rainy season in Israel, so they gave thanksgiving for the rain God would provide to soften the ground so that they could plow and plant crops. The spiritual significance referred to the Messiah who would give them living water. The priest took water in a golden pitcher from the pool of Siloam, and he gave it to the high priest who poured it at the foot of the altar. The priests blew their trumpets, and the Levites and the people waved palm branches while singing from Isaiah 12:3, "Therefore with joy you will draw water from the wells of salvation." It was a very joyous time and they sought God from Isaiah 44:3, asking Him to pour water on the dry ground.[11]

Jesus attended the feast, and as the high priest was pouring the water, Jesus made this statement, "On the last day, that great day of the feast, Jesus stood and cried out, saying, 'If anyone thirsts, let him come to Me and drink'" (John 7:37). Can you imagine how you would have felt attending the feast, praying for spiritual rain and the Messiah to come, and here a man gets up and says, *I will give you spiritual rain.* Jesus was either the Messiah or He was not in His right mind. No one

---
10. Dr. Richard Booker, *Celebrating Jesus in the Biblical Feasts: Discovering Their Significance to You as a Christian* (Shippensburg, PA: Destiny Image, 2008), 146.
11. Ibid.

else said some of the things Jesus said. "With this statement, Jesus was saying, 'Look unto Me and be saved now. I am the "Great Hosanna." I am your salvation. I will give the living waters of the Holy Spirit to all who receive Me as the true tabernacle of God.'"[12]

There was another ritual during the Feast of Tabernacles. Many of the pilgrims who came to the temple carried a torch which lighted the city. The significance of this was, "Plenty of sunshine was needed along with the rain to have a successful agricultural season. The Jews thanked God for the sun that was necessary for the life of the harvest. They also recognized that God Himself was the true Light (see Psalm 27:1) who would give them spiritual light and life through the Messiah."[13] Jesus made another bold statement, "I am the light of the world. He who follows Me shall not walk in darkness, but have the light of life" (John 8:12).

Let us come back to the ministry of Jesus. He traveled through Samaria and stopped at a well in the village of Sychar. Jews avoided this area, because they despised the Samaritans who lived there. Jesus rested at the well. He talked to a Samaritan woman who came to get water, and He asked her for a drink. She didn't understand. He was a Jew and she a Samaritan. Jews didn't ask Samaritans for water. Jesus offered her water and told her if she knew who was offering her water, she would ask Him for living water (John 4:10).

She still didn't understand, and Jesus continued that everyone who drank of this water would not ever be thirsty again. "But the water that I shall give him will become in him a fountain of water springing up into everlasting life" (John 4:14b). She still thought it was natural water and told Jesus she wanted this water that would cause her to never thirst again; then she wouldn't have to come and draw water every day. Jesus was revealing to her that He was the Messiah and that He could give her spiritual life. John 7:38-39 tells us the spiritual water is the Holy Spirit, who would be given after Jesus died and was resurrected and went to heaven.

---
12. Ibid.,147.
13. Dr. Richard Booker, *Celebrating Jesus in the Biblical Feasts: Discovering Their Significance to You as a Christian* (Shippensburg, PA: Destiny Image, 2008), 147.

She asked Jesus why the Samaritans worshiped at Mount Gerizim and the Jews insisted that Jerusalem was the only place where God should be worshiped. Jesus shared another secret with her. He told her the time would come when the place where people worshiped God would not be important, but whether they worshiped Him in Spirit and in truth. The focus on Mount Gerizim and Jerusalem brought separation and division. Jesus said what would become important was whether believers had His Spirit and came together with other believers who had His Spirit. When we worship, we can connect with the Holy Spirit. It is not just a ritual; it is a time of enjoying His presence. It is important to connect to a fellowship of believers where you feel welcomed and loved and where you can grow spiritually.

The woman at the well told him that when the Messiah came He would explain everything to them. Jesus did not hold back: "Then Jesus told her, 'I AM the Messiah!'" (John 4:26 NLT). What a bold statement. There are few people whom Jesus directly told that He was the Messiah, yet He shared this with a Samaritan woman. Jesus asked her to go and call her husband. When she said she didn't have a husband, Jesus told her she had had five husbands and the one she was living with was not her husband. She believed. She ran and told everyone in town about this man who told her everything she had ever done. Could He be the Messiah?

Holy-Spirit-empowered Jesus had an effect on everyone He met. He upset the Pharisees and Sadducees. He ate with sinners. People loved Him. Crowds flocked to Him. "Jesus traveled throughout the region of Galilee, teaching in the synagogues and announcing the Good News about the Kingdom. And he healed every kind of disease and illness. News about him spread as far as Syria, and people soon began bringing to him all who were sick. And whatever their sickness or disease, or if they were demon possessed or epileptic or paralyzed—he healed them all. Large crowds followed him wherever he went" (Matthew 4:23-25a NLT).

Discussion Questions: Jesus Starts His Ministry

1. Jesus started His ministry after He was baptized (Matthew 3:16-17). Name some things that happened in Jesus' ministry that can be attributed to the power of the Holy Spirit. Do you think we need the Holy Spirit today to be like Jesus?

   _____
   _____
   _____

2. Jesus called twelve disciples and told them "Come, follow me" (John 1:43 NLT). If you think about your life, can you say to someone, "Come, follow me"? Write down areas of strength and weakness that you need prayer for.

   _____
   _____
   _____
   _____

3. Who is our teacher today? (See John 14:16-17,26.) Share examples of how the Holy Spirit teaches you and works in your life.

   _____
   _____
   _____

4. Discuss what Jesus shared with Nicodemus in John 3:3-6 about being born twice. How does a person become born again? (See Romans 3:23; 1 John 1:9; Romans 10:9.)

   _____
   _____
   _____

5. When you gather with other believers, what do you consider when you have to decide which fellowship you want to join? The worship (singing/music), the message, statement of faith, or the fellowship?

6. Ponder the Word: Take some time and ponder one of the following Scriptures. Write down thoughts that come to mind around these Scriptures.

> "A new commandment I give to you, that you love one another; as I have loved you, that you also love one another. By this all will know that you are My disciples, if you have love for one another" (John 13:34-35).

> "Let all *that* you *do* be done with love" (1 Corinthians 16:14).

Chapter 4: The Teaching of Jesus

"And again He began to teach by the sea. And a great multitude was gathered to Him, so that He got into a boat and sat in it on the sea; and the whole multitude was on the land facing the sea" (Mark 4:1).

When we look at movies about Bible times the characters look foreign to us. They don't dress the way we do. They lived a simpler life without electricity and had different customs than what we have today. When we gain insight into some of the customs of those times, it can help us understand the Scriptures better. Jesus taught and traveled like the rabbis (religious teachers) of those days.

Jesus spoke to the crowds using stories or parables that people could relate to. He used situations that people were familiar with to teach spiritual truths. We also find that the disciples often asked Jesus what the parables meant after the crowds had dispersed (see Matthew 13:36). A parable can also be described as "an earthly story with a heavenly meaning." Jesus used examples from daily life to explain truth to the people; for example, a King would be a symbol for God (see Matthew 18:23-35; 22:2-14). Animal or nature parables were popular too (see Luke 9:58; Matthew 24:32). He told parables about a farmer (see Mark 4:1-32) and sheep (see Matthew 18:12; John 10). He used the grapevine as an example of how we should be connected to Him and receive life from Him in John chapter 15.

The disciples asked Jesus why he spoke to the crowds mostly in parables. Jesus answered that it was prophesied in the Scriptures that He would speak in parables (Matthew 13:34-35; Psalm 78:2-3). Jesus was fully God and fully man. As we read about Jesus, we see both in His life. We see Jesus walking the earth as a man fitting into the culture that He was born into. We also see His God nature when He healed people and spoke into their lives. John the Baptist said of Him, "For he is sent by God. He speaks God's words, for God gives him the Spirit without limit" (John 3:34 NLT). Jesus spoke as One who had authority, and people were amazed at His teaching (Mark 1:22). As you read about Jesus in the Bible, recognize where He operated—in the power of the Holy Spirit—when He did miracles, healed people, and had the right word at the right time to speak into a person's life. He interacted with people in a very natural way. When we receive Jesus we become His disciples. We receive His Spirit, and He is training us to walk the earth like He did, to bring His kingdom to the earth. He taught His disciples to pray that it would be on earth as it is in heaven (Matthew 6:10). Prayer opens the way for God to move on earth. He is not limited to prayer and can do anything at any time, but He chooses to move through people's prayers.

One of Jesus' most famous teachings is known as the Beatitudes:

> Blessed are the poor in spirit, for theirs is the kingdom of heaven.
>
> Blessed are those who mourn, for they shall be comforted.
>
> Blessed are the meek, for they shall inherit the earth.
>
> Blessed are those who hunger and thirst for righteousness, for they shall be filled.
>
> Blessed are the merciful, for they shall obtain mercy.
>
> Blessed are the pure in heart, for they shall see God.
>
> Blessed are the peacemakers, for they shall be called sons of God.
>
> Blessed are those who are persecuted for righteousness' sake, for theirs is the kingdom of heaven.
>
> Blessed are you when they revile and persecute you, and say all kinds of evil against you falsely for My sake (Matthew 5:3-11).

These Beatitudes reveal to us how to live life. They are a picture of humility, dependence upon God, and reacting in the opposite spirit. The world teaches a person to defend their rights, and there can be times when we need to do that, but I have learned that reacting in the opposite spirit has great power. When we encounter pride, we keep our hearts humble. Not a false humility or pretense, but humility from the heart. After all these years that I have walked with God I know how much I need Him daily. I know how much I need wisdom from the Holy Spirit in everything I do. I know God has the best solution for every situation I face. Walking in humility means to walk in dependence upon God and the leading of the Holy Spirit. The Bible teaches us to humble ourselves (James 4:10). If we don't humble ourselves, then God has to do it. Somewhere in life we will encounter a situation where we don't have the wisdom, knowledge, or strength necessary and we will find that we need God.

A time of sickness or difficulty, when our faith is tested, reveals how much faith we really have in God. My mother's battle with cancer revealed her childlike faith. In December 2012, she received devastating news—she had cancer, and the doctor gave her less than a month to live. Naturally she was shaken, but in the midst of the news she experienced the presence of the Holy Spirit around her like a blanket, giving her a supernatural sense of peace. She started to make peace with the fact that she wouldn't be on earth much longer. Two young people came to pray for her healing and she told them, "Don't pray for my healing, but rather pray that I don't have pain." This was too much to ask two young adults full of faith, and they told her, "Well, Grannie, then we will just pray that you will go to heaven healed," and they prayed for her healing. She got better, and through surgery the doctor removed the cancer. After the second surgery the doctor gave her bad news again—the cancer was back. She answered, "Doctor, my life is not in your hands; the number of my days is in the hand of God." The time came when she had to make a decision—chemo or surgery. The removal of an organ could save her life. The doctor told her to pray about it. A visit to the oncologist revealed chemo would not help. Next she went for a visit to the cardiologist to determine whether her heart was strong enough for a major surgery. She told the heart doctor, "If I die during surgery, then it is not your fault; it is God's time for me to die." She came through the surgery doing well, but a few days later she became very ill and received emergency surgery to clean out an infection which was a huge setback to her recovery.

What an example my mom was to me through all this, revealing her faith that no matter what happens, her life is in God's hands. I can see why the Bible says, "Assuredly, I say to you, whoever does not receive the kingdom of God as a little child will by no means enter it" (Mark 10:15). My mom had childlike faith. It was not a complicated faith. It was a trusting faith. In every circumstance, good or bad, she believed that her life was in God's hands and Jesus was walking with her through it. It reminds me of Psalm 23, "The Lord is my shepherd…even when I walk through the darkest valley, I will not be afraid, for you are close beside me. Your rod and your staff protect and comfort me" (Psalm 23:1a,4 NLT).

Sometimes ordinary people cross our paths. People like my mom. She was an ordinary woman with an extraordinary faith in God. Her God could never disappoint her. In life or death she was safe in His hands and she knew He would take care of her. I can see why her favorite psalm was Psalm 121: "I will lift up my eyes to the hills—from whence comes my help? My help comes from the Lord, who made heaven and earth" (Psalm 121:1-2).

During this difficult time I watched a song on the Internet based on Psalm 103:1: "Bless the Lord, O my soul; and all that is within me, *bless* His holy name!" I realized what a secure place it is that we find ourselves in, if we can say, "Bless the Lord, O my soul," no matter what the circumstances are. I can sing it when life is going well and I can sing it with truth and conviction even in difficult times, trusting that Jesus whom I received into my heart is the One walking with me and helping me through every situation. It doesn't mean that there won't be any challenges, but we have a Helper, the Holy Spirit, who knows us and every circumstance. I have experienced how He has given me inner strength and peace during the difficult time of my mother's illness.

God wants to be involved in every area of our lives. Just like the Beatitudes, no matter what circumstances we face, whether we are poor or rich, blessed or persecuted, God wants us to live in dependence upon Him and involve Him in every area of our lives. "Look at the birds of the air, for they neither sow nor reap nor gather into barns; yet your heavenly Father feeds them. Are you not of more value than they?" (Matthew 6:26).

In the Jewish culture they prayed short prayers of blessing throughout the day. "Nowadays the ancient blessings said upon awakening are prayed during the morning prayer service. The very first words on the lips of the Jews are these: 'I am grateful before You, living and eternal King, for returning my soul to me with compassion. You are faithful beyond measure.'"[14] What a wonderful tradition. I can see how it would set our focus on God if we started our days like that. It reminds me of the first commandment God gave Israel—to love the Lord your God with all your heart, mind, and soul (Deuteronomy 6:5). Those words, "I am grateful before You…You are faithful beyond measure," immediately bring an attitude of thankfulness. What a great way to start a day. "Rejoice always, pray without ceasing, in everything give thanks; for this is the will of God in Christ Jesus for you" (1 Thessalonians 5:16-18).

Looking at the Beatitudes along with the cultural tradition of speaking multiple blessings during the day, we can see Jesus was telling the people to bless God no matter what happens. When life goes well or when we are facing challenges or persecution, continue to bless God. It will bring heavenly reward. I spent time with my mom when she was very sick in the hospital—she was on a ventilator, dialysis, and had tubes everywhere. The tubes of the ventilator hurt her mouth so much that she had sores all over her mouth and lips. She was very weak and in bad shape. I prayed for her every time I visited her. I read and prayed Scriptures to her, focusing on Psalm 23 and Psalm 139. While I was reading and praying Psalm 23:6, "Surely goodness and mercy shall follow me all the days of my life," I was thinking, *this is a horrible situation for her. She always said God has been good to her throughout her life. He helped her through every situation in her life. How can I still proclaim this Scripture?* But I just felt the faith and the prompting of the

---

14. Ann Spangler and Lois Tverberg, *Sitting at the Feet of Rabbi Jesus: How the Jewishness of Jesus Can Transform Your Faith* (Grand Rapids, MI: Zondervan, 2009), 93. Used by Permission of Zondervan. www.Zondervan.com.

Holy Spirit that God was faithful and He would reveal His goodness and His mercy even in this situation.

When Jesus came to earth He didn't just appear from heaven, looking different from the rest of us. He didn't come fully equipped and already made to be the Savior of the world. He came to earth, born as a baby, and walked the earth as a man, "made Himself of no reputation, taking the form of a bondservant, and coming in the likeness of men" (Philippians 2:7). Jesus humbled Himself; He learned obedience to earthly parents and walked in obedience to His heavenly Father, obeying even unto death on the cross.

The Word (Jesus) became flesh in a human body and He walked it out on earth. "After Jesus had received the 'fullness' of the Spirit in the Jordan, He was led into the wilderness for a time of testing and proving. Here, the Word became 'power' in His life. Now, when Jesus ministered, men became attentive and said, *'Never man spoke like this Man'* (John 7:46). Why? Because the Word and the flesh (His life experience) had become one. This is the oneness which the Lord desires to work in our lives."[15] We hear the Word and receive it, but it doesn't help us much if it doesn't become life experience. The challenging part is walking it out. Jesus experienced temptations and He overcame them. It wasn't just a message He shared—the message had power. Jesus was obedient to God, and God released authority on His words. One of the biggest challenges we will face is to forgive time and again. Jesus forgave even in the midst of death. The gospel message doesn't mean much if we just preach it; we must live it too.

When Moses received the Law, the people started to focus on the Law and tried to earn their salvation by trying to obey every law. They missed the point. The Law reveals to us what sin is (Romans 7:7). It shows us the right way to live. It causes us to realize that no matter how hard we try, we cannot fulfill the Law perfectly; we need a Savior. Instead, many Pharisees and Sadducees tried to fulfill the Law, making more laws and interpreting the laws, and so tried to live a life that would

---

15. Wade E. Taylor, *Waterspouts of Glory, Volume One* (Greensboro, NC: Wade Taylor Publications, 1995), 51.

be acceptable to God. Hebrews 10:16 tells us that in the new covenant God writes His laws on our hearts and minds. We read and study the Bible; and at the time we need the truth of a Scripture, the Holy Spirit brings it to remembrance. I have often turned to a Scripture or a passage on the exact day that I needed it.

The disciples asked Jesus to teach them how to pray. Jesus taught them to say, "Our Father in heaven" (Matthew 6:9). Jesus called God *Father* or *Abba*. He had the revelation that God was His Father. Our son, Estian, went on a mission trip with a group of students. They were driving to Colorado, and he wasn't even an hour into the trip when his car broke down. He was very upset and disappointed. The first thing he did was call his dad. "Dad, help, what should I do?" Isn't it good to have a Daddy in heaven who knows how to deal with every problem we encounter? I have found that in a crisis situation there is usually a progressive, unfolding series of events. In this instance, the car broke down. My son and his friends managed to get it towed it to the closest town. There he received bad news; the whole engine needed to be replaced. He decided to continue on the mission trip and then to deal with the car situation when he got back. Our other son, Morgan, went to Philadelphia for a mission trip; he could pick up my car (I was in South Africa at the time) and take it to where Estian was. Every step of the way, we solved the problem by praying, more praying, and asking God how to fix the situation. We didn't have extra money, and my son had a little bit saved up. Eventually he got the car fixed. His savings were enough to fix it. It was at this time that he decided to go to Thailand on another mission trip and had planned to use part of his savings for that trip. God showed Himself faithful to our son and provided for the Thailand trip.

Jesus often spent time in prayer, "He went out to the mountain to pray, and continued all night in prayer to God" (Luke 6:12b). Jesus knew where His strength came from. He modeled how to live life in dependence upon God while He walked the earth. He didn't act by Himself; He acted by the authority of God, "The words that I speak to you I do not speak on My own authority; but the Father who dwells in Me does the works" (John 14:10b). When people heard of the miracles of Jesus, it drew huge crowds. During the day Jesus taught in the temple, and in the evenings He spent time with His Father. He often spent time with God in the garden on the Mount of Olives (Luke 21:37). If Jesus needed to spend time with His Father, how much more do I need to spend time with my heavenly Father? I cannot act in my own strength and just do things because I think they are the best things to do.

When Jesus taught the disciples to pray, He told them to ask God for their daily bread. Most of the people living in a western world don't have a lack of food. This prayer for our daily food shows me that we can trust God for our most basic needs. If I can trust Him for food, I can trust Him to help me to get my car fixed and make wise decisions about everything He has given me stewardship over.

Jesus also addressed forgiveness. "And forgive us our debts, as we forgive our debtors" (Matthew 6:12). He told a parable about forgiveness. He talked about a king who wanted to settle his accounts. The king forgave a servant who owed him a lot of money. That servant left the king's presence and on his way he found someone who owed him money. He was not as forgiving as the king; he demanded the money, and when the man couldn't pay he let the man be thrown in jail. The king heard what this servant did and called him in and said he had had mercy on the servant for not paying his debt; shouldn't the servant do the same? Then the king ordered the servant to be delivered to the torturers until he could pay the debt (Matthew 18:23-35). The key to this parable is in verse 35: "So My heavenly Father also will do to you if each of you, from his heart, does not forgive his brother his trespasses."

When we forgive someone else it sets us free. The person is still accountable to God for what he or she did. When I forgive, *I* am set free. Unforgiveness causes people to experience what verse 34 talks about—being delivered to the torturers. Those are spiritual torturers; it can be depression or sickness. In Acts 8 we read about Simon, who practiced sorcery. Saul told him that his heart was poisoned by bitterness (Acts 8:23). We were not designed to carry offenses and unforgiveness (Ephesians 4:31; Hebrews 12:15). We were designed by God to live free in daily thankfulness and joy toward God.

I never realized how easily I judged others. It wasn't long after I turned my life over to Jesus that He started to deal with me about this. He wanted more from me than just outward obedience. Many people who do not follow Jesus obey the laws of the land and live a good life. Jesus said of the Pharisees that they honored God with their words, but their hearts were far from Him. In my walk with Jesus through the years, He dealt with my heart time and again. He wasn't satisfied that I was outwardly doing the right thing. He wanted my heart to be right with God and other people. So He showed me when I judged someone or when I was offended or hurt, and He helped me to deal appropriately with the sinful responses of my heart.

Jesus gave the example of a house built upon sand and a house built upon a rock. "Therefore whoever hears these sayings of Mine, and does them, I will liken him to a wise man who built his house on the rock" (Matthew 7:24). The man who built his house upon the sandy ground, his house was washed away. Following Jesus requires more than just giving Him your heart. He desires your whole heart, your affections, your thinking, and your response to every situation. The good news is I don't have to do this struggling in my own strength. As I spend time with Him and turn to Him, His Spirit works in my heart and changes me and shows me the areas where I need to change.

Discussion Questions: The Teaching of Jesus

1. There was a difference between the teachings of Jesus and the religious leaders (Mark 1:22). What do you think was the difference and why?

2. The Beatitudes reveal a different kind of blessing that is opposite to the culture we live in (Matthew 5:3-11). Think of examples of how to react in the opposite spirit when you encounter evil, for example—slander, accusation, or criticism.

3. It takes a strong faith in God to say in a challenging situation, "Bless the Lord, O my soul; and all that is within me, bless His holy name! (Psalm 103:1). Do you have any helpful suggestions that could help a person who is going through a difficult situation?

4. Forgiveness is not always easy. Why is it important to forgive? (Matthew 18:23-35)

5. Rejoicing and blessing:

   a) Share ideas how can we practice this verse: "Rejoice always, pray without ceasing, in everything give thanks; for this is the will of God in Christ Jesus for you" (1 Thessalonians 5:16-18).

   _____
   _____
   _____

   b) What difference would it make in your life if you focused on continually blessing God as the Jewish custom of blessing portrays?

   _____
   _____
   _____

6. Ponder the Word: Choose one of the Beatitudes and ask the Holy Spirit to speak to you about it. Write down thoughts that come to your mind (Matthew 5:3-11).

   _____
   _____
   _____
   _____
   _____

Chapter 5: The Kingdom of Heaven

> "From that time Jesus began to preach and to say, 'Repent, for the kingdom of heaven is at hand'" (Matthew 4:17)

John the Baptist came preaching—*repent, for the kingdom of heaven is at hand*. He was the messenger Isaiah prophesied would prepare the way before Jesus (Isaiah 40:3). Jesus shared the same message as John the Baptist, and His disciples baptized people as they repented (Luke 3:12; John 3:22). *Repent* means to change the mind, or the course of conduct, on account of regret or dissatisfaction; to be sorry for sin as morally evil, to turn from it, and seek forgiveness.[16] "For godly sorrow produces repentance leading to salvation" (2 Corinthians 7:10a).

What did Jesus mean when He talked about the kingdom of heaven? Where is the kingdom of heaven? When we ask someone, "Where does God live?" the answer we often will receive is, "In heaven." What does the Bible tell us about heaven? We see that the area where the sun, moon, and stars are located is called *heaven* or *the heavens*. But we also read about a spiritual *heaven*. Jacob dreamed about a stairway that reached up to heaven and angels were going up and down the stairway. At the top of the stairway he saw the Lord, who then spoke to Jacob (Genesis 28:12).

Even though God is omnipresent, we also know that there is a place called *heaven* that is God's dwelling place. "Now look down from your holy dwelling place in heaven" (Deuteronomy 26:15a NLT). John, one of Jesus' disciples, was on the island of Patmos when he saw a vision of a door standing open in heaven. He also saw the throne room and

---

16. *Webster's Collegiate Dictionary*, s.v., "repent."

someone sitting on a throne, shining as beautiful gemstones (Revelation 4:1-3). Revelation 19:7-9 tells us about the wedding feast of Jesus which will take place in heaven. Heaven is the kingdom where there will be no more tears, sickness, or death. The struggles that we deal with on earth will pass away as we enter heaven (Revelation 21:4).

Jesus taught His disciples to pray, "Your kingdom come. Your will be done on earth as it is in heaven" (Matthew 6:10). In heaven there is no sickness, no disease, no hurt or pain. Jesus healed many people during the three years of His ministry. He brought the kingdom of heaven, the kingdom of God to them. Every time a person was healed, the kingdom of heaven broke in and manifested on earth. When Jesus ministered to someone and the person was healed or delivered, the kingdom of heaven manifested in that person's life. This is for every person who follows Jesus' mandate—to pray for situations and let God break in from the realm of eternity into our physical earthly realm and change the situation. God doesn't always respond the way we want, but He always works every situation for our good. Even at times when God didn't answer the way I expected, I can look back and say He was good to me in the situation and He knew best.

I have a wonderful friend who walked through a very difficult year. She had several crisis situations, and we often prayed together about them. She saw God break in and work on her behalf time and again. She saw breakthrough in situations that were seemingly impossible. If I look at her life, I see the faithfulness of God over and over. That is her testimony, and that is what God wants to do for us. He is an ever present help in time of need. We just need to ask.

Jesus talked about the kingdom of heaven and compared it to something of great value. He told the parable of a man who found a treasure buried in a field. He went and sold everything he had and bought that field. Jesus said here that if you find the kingdom of heaven, you find the best treasure of all (Matthew 13:44). After more than twenty years of following Jesus, there is no doubt in my mind—to find Jesus, to walk in relationship with God and learn about God's kingdom principles, exceeds every earthly treasure you could ever have. My experience has been that in life people will hurt you, disappoint you, and not always treat you fairly. What has kept me time and again was my personal relationship with Jesus. He is more important to me than anything else. When I get hurt or am disappointed, I run to Jesus. He is my safe haven. "The name of the Lord is a strong tower; the righteous run to it and are safe" (Proverbs 18:10).

Jesus reinforced the parable about the kingdom of heaven with a second parable about a merchant seeking a pearl. When the merchant found this very precious pearl, he sold everything he had and bought it (Matthew 13:45-46). In both situations, the people went and sold everything they had to buy the treasure or the pearl. Jesus said the same thing to the rich man when the man asked him how he can enter the kingdom of heaven (Mark 10:21-23). Following Jesus with a whole heart will cost you everything. This doesn't mean that we should not own anything; it means our possessions should not be our idols or stand in the way of our following God wholeheartedly.

In 1999, we left our home country of South Africa to move to the USA. We downsized until everything we owned fit into a few suitcases. The first few months in the USA, I realized it would be very easy to just pack up and follow God wherever He led, because we had nothing that tied us down. Eventually we settled down, bought a house, and filled it. Around 2006, I went through a test about our earthly possessions again. Our permanent residence status was taking a long time to come through, our visas were expiring, and I wondered what we would do if we had to go back to South Africa. That whole week I was looking at the furniture we accumulated and thought about what I would take and what I would leave. By the end of the week, I knew that if that happened, we would leave the country with a few suitcases. None of our possessions were so valuable that I felt like I had to take them with me. When I got to the point that I released everything we owned, our paperwork came through. It is very freeing if our earthly stuff doesn't have a hold on us. Jesus wants to be Lord over every part of our lives.

Jesus told a parable in which He compared people hearing the Word of God with seed being sown. He shared four different scenarios of what could happen to this seed. The birds could come and eat it, the seed could fall on rocky ground, it could be choked by weeds, or it could fall in good ground. The disciples asked Jesus what this meant. He explained it to them. When someone hears the Word and they do not understand it, demonic spirits (birds of the air) come and snatch it away.

The rocky areas are hardened hearts—when the Word comes, the person receives the seed with joy, but because of a hardened heart it does not take root. Our hearts can be hardened because of bitterness, offenses, judgments, criticism, or negativity. Someone who sits and listens to a message with a critical or judgmental ear does not receive much from the greatest message. The good news is that when we open our hearts and repent of those "hard" areas—whether it is bitterness, an offense, criticism, or negativity—the soil of our hearts can become good ground for the Word of the kingdom to be sown, ground that will bring forth a harvest (Matthew 13:18-23).

The weeds represent the cares of this world that choke out the Word. Think about it this way. If someone constantly thinks about their cares and worries, it is hard to be open to hear what God is saying. The Bible tells us to cast our cares upon God (1 Peter 5:7). Just as I found the freedom to travel light in the natural, I also travel light in my spirit. I try to release the cares of this world to God, not to hold on to grudges or offenses, and to walk in God's peace.

Jesus also compared the kingdom of heaven with a farmer sowing good seeds. During the night while the farmer was sleeping, the enemy came and sowed tares amongst the wheat (Matthew 13:24-30). The disciples asked Jesus to explain the parable to them. Jesus told them the enemy who sows the weeds is the Devil. The good seed represents those who belong to the kingdom of heaven. Both of these seeds grow together until the end of the age when God will send His angels to reap the harvest. The weeds will be thrown into the fire and the wheat will shine in their Father's kingdom.

The seeds are sown in our hearts. One day as I was just resting in the presence of God listening to worship music I saw a vision. I saw black seeds in my heart and an angel taking them out and replacing them with golden seeds. Then I saw these golden seeds sprout and green plants appear. I wondered about this. Think about seeds. If we say hurtful or negative words, those would be bad seed. When I encourage and bless others with my words, they have a positive effect and bring forth fruit and blessing. The seed that God sows in our lives will bring forth encouragement and blessing. I need to make room in my heart for the good seed. If my heart is full of negative and critical feelings, there is no room to receive the good. When I repent of those negative feelings or thoughts, I cleanse my heart and make room to receive the good words and plans from God.

As a young Christian, the Holy Spirit showed me how quickly I judged someone through the lens of my own experience. He showed me that I don't have all the information about another person's situation and I don't know why the person acted the way they did. I needed to keep my mouth closed and not judge (Matthew 7:1-2). If it is something that is outright wrong, then I can know it is wrong, but I should not share it with others. I should keep my mouth closed unless I am in a leadership position or it is a situation where God or the law requires that I do something. Other than that, my responsibility is to pray for the person. When I talk about the sins of others, it is slander and tears the person down. Jesus loves this person and His desire is for repentance and restoration. "Let him know that he who turns a sinner from the error of his way will save a soul from death and cover a multitude of sins" (James 5:20). The problem is not when we talk in earnest with someone who did something wrong. The damage is done when people start to spread rumors and form judgments. This is not helpful to anyone and does not help to solve the initial problem.

Many years ago while we were praying for unity between churches, I saw a vision. I saw a brick wall that was about the height of a person. In my mind I heard a song that I had been listening to that week about breaking dividing walls. In the vision I saw people taking one brick at a time and carrying it away. They threw them in the ocean. I realized those bricks represented the judgments and offenses we as Christians carry against each other. When we repent of those judgments, we are tearing the brick wall down. I didn't know there was a Scripture that would confirm this, but the next day I stumbled upon it: "You will cast all our sins into the depths of the sea" (Micah 7:19). As we repent of the things that divide us, those walls are broken down.

Jesus compared the kingdom of heaven to a mustard seed. This is a very tiny seed that becomes a huge tree (Matthew 13:31-32). He also compared it to leaven, or yeast. Leaven causes dough to rise, so it is increased (Matthew 13:33). Both the parable of the mustard seed and the leaven reveal to us that there is an increase wherever the kingdom of God or the kingdom of heaven manifest. When people come to know Jesus, truth multiplies; when people are healed, the kingdom of God manifests; when those in need receive help and food, the kingdom of God increases. The religious leaders wanted to stop Jesus' influence two thousand years ago. They thought if He was killed His influence would cease. The kingdom of heaven has advanced since Jesus died. Multiplication and increase are kingdom principles. The opposite happens when people slander, gossip, judge, and get offended with each other. These practices kill spiritual growth.

The disciples asked Jesus in Matthew 18:1-4 who was the greatest in the kingdom. In the western world we are often impressed with a person's position or what people own. "Wow, he's a senator," or, "You should see his car." The disciples wanted to know which of them would hold the greatest position in heaven. Jesus did not respond as they expected. He called a little child and told the people that if they don't turn from their sins and become like little children, they would not be able to get into heaven. What was Jesus saying? *Be like a child*—a child is without pretense. Be open, be humble, and be real. God knows everything about us. He knows our thoughts even before we think them. There is no point in wearing a mask. He sees through it. It won't help to try and hide anything from Him.

David poured out his heart and struggles to God, and then He turned them into praise. God can handle my honesty, because He made a way for me to come clean. If I find myself thinking a negative or critical thought, I say, "I am sorry, Lord. I release this situation into Your hands. I ask You to be the judge of this situation. Cleanse my heart and wash me clean." Surrender at the cross. Lay it down and walk away in freedom. I am so thankful for the cross and what Jesus has done. Because of what Jesus has done, I can walk in freedom. I can have joy and have His supernatural peace in my life. I often find my way to the cross, just as we take a daily bath or shower and wash our hands regularly. I don't have to wait until evening. I just deal with it right away. I tell Jesus I am sorry for my negative thoughts and take them to the cross and leave them there.

After the disciples quarreled on the road about which of them was the most important, Jesus responded, "Whoever wants to be first must take last place and be the servant of everyone else" (Mark 9:35 NLT). The kingdom of heaven functions on different principles than earthly kingdoms where men vie for position. I didn't realize it, but during the twenty-four years when I was raising kids some of my identity became wrapped up in my role as a mother. When I was finished with raising our children, I went through a bit of an empty nest crisis. I wondered what I would do with my time; I did not feel qualified for anything. I had been out of the marketplace for so long that my job applications didn't go anywhere. I had to get my identity established in God's love for me. If God is my Daddy and Jesus is my best friend and He has sent me a Helper, the Holy Spirit, then He has something that I can do with my life. God has been so faithful that He even sent me a prophetic word about writing—something that I didn't think I could do but was encouraged to begin.

God has exalted Jesus to the highest position in the universe next to Himself. Every person will bow the knee eventually before Jesus (Philippians 2:6-11). When Jesus died on the cross for the forgiveness of our sins, it took away the power of the enemy. "Then God made you alive with Christ, for he forgave all our sins. He canceled the record of the charges against us and took it away by nailing it to the cross. In this way, he disarmed the spiritual rulers and authorities. He shamed them publicly by his victory over them on the cross" (Colossians 2:13b-15 NLT). Repentance disarms the enemy. It takes away his ammunition against us. I quickly repent when I have done something wrong. I do not want to give any demonic spirits ammunition against me.

I have personally seen the power of repentance many times in my life and in the lives of those around me. I have a friend who is a lawyer. Once he was defending a client who made a mistake and as a result, a young girl was killed in a car accident. The man came to a sorrowful repentance of what he did. He asked if he could talk to the mother of this girl and the girl's friend. They arranged the meeting. The young man came in and kneeled before the woman and told her how sorry he was about everything that had happened. The mom was just weeping; she couldn't get out a word. The girl's friend just sat there, not wanting to forgive the young man. They ended the meeting and went to the courtroom. The judge had mercy on the man, and he was sentenced to house arrest and community service. After the court proceedings, the mother came up to this man and said, "I have forgiven you; now you have to forgive yourself." What a beautiful picture of reconciliation and restoration. What happened that morning set that young man and the mother of the girl free in the spirit. The friend who didn't forgive will live under that yoke of bitterness until she forgives.

When John saw Jesus in the vision in Revelation, Jesus said, "I am the living one. I died, but look—I am alive forever and ever! And I hold the keys of death and the grave" (Revelation 1:18 NLT). The Pharisees wanted to know by whose authority Jesus was doing miracles. "Jesus came and told his disciples, 'I have been given all authority in heaven and on earth'" (Matthew 28:18 NLT). He was not acting in His own authority. He modeled the way for us by acting upon what His Father told Him to do and walking in the delegated authority that God the Father had given Him. "I don't speak on my own authority. The Father who sent me has commanded me what to say and how to say it" (John 12:49 NLT). Jesus lived in submission to God the Father, and He obeyed what God told Him to do. Jesus gave His disciples the authority to cast out evil spirits and to heal the sick (Matthew 10:1). The kingdom of heaven is about multiplication. Jesus trained up disciples, and before He left the earth He told His disciples to go and do the same. Jesus delegated His authority to the disciples and told them to go and make disciples. Every believer in Jesus is called to be a disciple who will walk in His delegated authority. Obedience is the character trait of a disciple.

In the days of Jesus they understood authority. The Pharisees, the people, and the Roman government wanted to know from whom Jesus received the authority to do miracles. The Roman officer told Jesus he believed Jesus could speak the word and his son would be healed. He said he was in a position of authority over soldiers and he knew how authority worked (Luke 7:8). Jesus taught with authority (Matthew 7:29). Jesus said God had given Him the authority to judge (John 5:22). He also had the authority to forgive sins (Matthew 9:6; Mark 2:10). There are things that are only in God the Father's hands. We see that times and seasons are in God's hand. Jesus said that God the Father has the authority to set the dates and times of events (Acts 1:7). Jesus doesn't know the date of His return; only God the Father knows when that will be (Matthew 24:36).

Jesus operated under His Father's authority. When the disciples were commanded not to speak about Jesus, they obeyed a higher authority. "But Peter and the apostles replied, 'We must obey God rather than any human authority'" (Acts 5:29 NLT). Jesus taught His followers to pay taxes and be obedient to the government. When it comes to a decision such as what Daniel and his friends faced, to place something or someone above God, then the Holy Spirit in us will say, "No, that is not right" (see Daniel 1 and 3).

Jesus told Peter that the powers of hell would not overcome His church. He spoke about the keys of the kingdom. "I will give you the keys of the kingdom of heaven; and whatever you bind (declare to be improper and unlawful) on earth must be what is already bound in heaven; and whatever you loose (declare lawful) on earth must be what is already loosed in heaven" (Matthew 16:19 AMP). God gave each one of us a sphere of authority. The Roman officer had authority over a group of men. Where you work you are given authority or responsibility over a certain task or people. Leaders of a country are given authority and responsibility over those who live in the country. They can make decisions that can bless the people or hurt the people. I can see why the Bible tells us to pray for those in authority (1 Timothy 2:1-2).

In my journey in life, during every challenging situation I kept pressing in. I knew God had the answer to every problem. He knew the solution. In some situations it took much longer to break through and other situations were easier. In every situation the answer was the same—pressing in to God, calling out to Him, praying to Him, and asking Him for wisdom and help. Then I continued to walk with Him and pray and work toward what He revealed.

Knowing Jesus has transformed my life. The good news of Jesus Christ is still transforming lives today. "This same Good News that came to you is going out all over the world. It is bearing fruit everywhere by changing lives, just as it changed your lives from the day you first heard and understood the truth about God's wonderful grace" (Colossians 1:6 NLT).

Discussion Questions: The Kingdom of Heaven

1. The message of John the Baptist was, "Repent, for the kingdom of heaven is at hand!" (Matthew 3:2). What is the importance of repentance in the Christian life?

2. Jesus taught the disciples to pray, "Your kingdom come. Your will be done on earth as it is in heaven" (Matthew 6:10). Write down situations where you have seen heaven come to earth—when you received answer to prayer. List some things that you need God's help with currently.

3: How do you pray for a situation when you don't have faith that God will do anything to change the situation?

4. Do you have any helpful suggestions about how to deal with a situation that feels overwhelming, and you don't know what to do or what to pray?

5. Jesus asked the rich young man to give up his earthly possessions. Take a moment and think how it would impact you if you lost all your possessions due to a natural disaster. Which possessions do you value the most? (If we really think about the impact this would have, we will have more compassion for those who are suffering.)

_____
_____
_____

6. Pondering the Word: Take a word or phrase from Colossians 1:9-11 or Colossians 2:6-7 and focus on it. Write down any thoughts that come to you as you spend time listening to what God is saying to you through this Scripture. The Living Bible reads, "And now just as you trusted Christ to save you, trust him, too, for each day's problems; live in vital union with him. Let your roots grow down deep into him and draw up nourishment from Him" (Colossians 2:6-7 TLB).

_____
_____
_____
_____
_____
_____
_____
_____

Chapter 6: Healing the Sick

"The Spirit of the Lord is upon Me, because He has anointed Me to preach the gospel to the poor; He has sent Me to heal the brokenhearted, to proclaim liberty to the captives and recovery of sight to the blind, to set at liberty those who are oppressed; to proclaim the acceptable year of the Lord" (Luke 4:18-19).

What would be the most impressive miracle you could witness? Many would say someone being raised from the dead; others might say someone in a wheelchair walking again or blind eyes opened. I watched a DVD clip of a man who ministered during the healing revival of the 1950s. He laid hands on a person who was terminally ill with stomach cancer. The man was just skin and bones. He had not been able to eat properly for the last six months prior to being carried into the meeting. I saw this healing evangelist as he laid his hands on this man and prayed for him in the name of Jesus and the man got up; he ate a sandwich and drank some milk. It was an amazing miracle. Only God can heal a man in such a terrible condition.

In several Scriptures we read that Jesus felt compassion for the people and He healed them. "And when Jesus went out He saw a great multitude; and He was moved with compassion for them, and healed their sick" (Matthew 14:14). If you look at the root word for *compassion*, it means being "moved in the bowels,"[17] which is the stomach area, meaning Jesus was stirred or moved in His spirit with compassion. "Then Jesus,

---

17. Thayer and Smith, "Greek Lexicon entry for Splagchnizomai," The NAS New Testament Greek Lexicon, accessed July 14, 2014, http://www.biblestudytools.com/lexicons/greek/nas/splagchnizomai.html.

moved with compassion, stretched out His hand and touched him, and said to him, 'I am willing; be cleansed'" (Mark 1:41).

Early in my walk with Jesus I learned that we not only receive salvation through the cross, but we also receive healing. "By his wounds you are healed" (1 Peter 2:24b NLT; see Isaiah 53:5). When someone in our family was sick, we prayed, and often God healed the person; sometimes it was a quick healing. Other times the healing was gradual, but quicker than normally expected, and there were times we had to go to the doctor for medicine. One day one of our sons sprained his ankle and his brother and I prayed for him before he got in bed that night. The praying brother saw a vision of an angel coming and working on the ankle. The next morning my son woke up and his ankle was fine. Another time someone ran into my son's knee in a soccer game. His knee was very swollen and he had to use crutches. We prayed for the knee, but it didn't seem to help. A few days later, I was invited to a prayer meeting and I took my son with me. At the end of the meeting the lady in charge asked my son if they could pray for him. While they prayed for him, she saw a vision and said, "I see a boy on the other team who said, 'I wish he would get hurt,' and it worked like a curse." This was quite a surprise to me, but then I remembered how many of his teammates had been hurt—one broke his toe, and my other son on the same team rode his bike into a truck and hurt his hip. There were many kids who were injured on the team, and this was a recreational league where the kids usually didn't get hurt. They prayed for his knee and it started to improve much quicker.

As I was writing this chapter, I found myself in the midst of a most difficult time in my life. I was daily visiting my mom, who has been in the ICU for more than a month. Many people were praying for her, and I prayed for her every time I was at the hospital. Three weeks ago, her kidneys improved so much that she was able to get off dialysis. As she was improving, she had a setback and contracted pneumonia. It had been such a hard uphill battle. She couldn't move or speak because of the tubes in her throat. She was conscious and it was very hard to see her so helpless. I experienced a situation where I prayed and prayed and prayed. I would see some breakthrough, but then there was a setback.

After fifty days of struggling, she went home to be with Jesus. Even though Jesus didn't heal her, I had peace. I knew my mom knew Him and she was in a better place, free from her earthly battles.

Even though the outcome with my mom's situation has not been as I would have liked, I have seen God's healing power enough in other times to still believe that He heals. Jesus said, "Most assuredly, I say to you, he who believes in Me, the works that I do he will do also; and greater works than these he will do, because I go to My Father" (John 14:12). We can make a difference as we pray. My husband and I went to the hospital to pray for someone. The man was on disability and the doctors said this man needed a liver transplant. We prayed for him, and other people also prayed. It was so encouraging to see the man a few months later as he returned to work—no longer in need of a liver transplant!

Jesus walked in the healing power of God in relationship with His Father. He said, "Do you not believe that I am in the Father, and the Father in Me? The words that I speak to you I do not speak on My own authority; but the Father who dwells in Me does the works" (John 14:10). Jesus healed every sickness that was known to their time. We don't read of any sickness that Jesus couldn't heal. He healed leprosy, which was incurable at that time. In Matthew 8:2-4, this leper said, "Lord, if You are willing, You can make me clean." We do not read of one account where a person asked Jesus to heal him and Jesus said no. When the ten lepers asked Jesus to heal them, Jesus told them to show themselves to the priests and as they were on their way they were healed (Luke 17:11-19). In this situation they had to act upon what Jesus told them.

When we visited our family in South Africa, they made us feel welcome and prepared wonderful meals for us. It was such a comforting, warm feeling to be so welcomed by our family. This made me realize how wonderful it feels to be welcomed, compared to situations where I had felt not welcomed or received. When people don't receive us, we do not want to open ourselves up and give of ourselves. I have noticed that I can receive a message from a person who is preaching even though it might not be my preferred preaching style. Then, too, I have been with others who did not receive anything at all from a meeting because they didn't like the preaching style. When we keep our hearts open we receive more. When my son was in high school, he went to a church meeting with a friend. The preacher said something about the end times that was different than my son had been taught. I was blessed when my son said that he decided that it was not going to hinder him from receiving what God wanted to speak to him through this man that evening. Later he said, "Mom, I did receive something from the Lord." God can speak in many ways through many different situations and people if we are just open to receive and hear from Him.

The only time that we read of a time when Jesus could not do many miracles was when He was not honored in His hometown. This happened in Nazareth. Jesus taught in the synagogue, and people were amazed at His teaching. Then they suddenly remembered who Jesus was. He was Joseph the carpenter's son. Mary was His mother, and they knew His brothers and sisters. "And they were deeply offended and refused to believe in him. Then Jesus told them, 'A prophet is honored everywhere except in his own hometown and among his own family.' And so he did only a few miracles there because of their unbelief" (Matthew 13:57-58 NLT). How sad! They had Jesus in their midst; at first they had recognized His authority in the Spirit, but then they looked at Him in the flesh and missed their moment of visitation.

Think about giving honor. In a situation where you are not welcomed and received, how do you feel? You don't feel like you want to share your gifts and your talents in an environment where you are not welcomed. It makes it difficult for a person to enjoy what they are doing and give their best if they are not valued. On the other hand, in a situation where people respect you and recognize the gifts and talents that God has placed in you and make room for you to walk in them, you bloom like a flower opening up. We function best when we are welcomed and received.

Jesus healed many people. In some situations, we see Jesus cast out a demon and the person was healed. A blind and mute man was brought to Jesus. The demons started to react in Jesus' presence. They acknowledged that Jesus was the Son of God. Jesus didn't waste time;

He addressed the demons, "Be quiet, and come out of him!" (Luke 4:35 NLT). The demons threw the man on the ground and left. The people who saw this were amazed. "What authority and power this man's words possess! Even evil spirits obey Him, and they flee at His command" (Luke 4:36 NLT). It caused such a stir that the news of Jesus' ministry spread through the entire region.

I heard of an account of a man who helped in the ministry of one of the 1950s healing evangelists. He and another man tried to pray for someone to be set free from a demonic spirit. They couldn't do it. They called the evangelist. He bent down and whispered in the man's ear. The demon left. They were surprised and asked him what he said. He told them, "I said—Devil, this is…" and said his name. This evangelist knew whose authority he was walking in. When we know the One in whose authority we walk, we will have faith and confidence. It is not just about using our authority; it is about knowing Him.

When Jesus was in Cana, a government official who lived in Capernaum came and asked Jesus to heal his son who was sick. Jesus told the man to go home; his son would live. The man believed Jesus and on his way he met some of his servants who told him his son was well. When the man asked them when his son had been healed, he heard that it was at the exact time Jesus had told him that his son would be healed. Jesus could speak and the healing happened!

One evening Jesus arrived at Peter's house, where He found that Peter's mother-in-law was sick with a high fever. Jesus just touched her hand and the fever left her body and she was well. She got out of bed and prepared food for them (Matthew 8:14-15). "That evening many demon-possessed people were brought to Jesus. He cast out the evil spirits with a simple command, and he healed all the sick" (Matthew 8:16 NLT). Sometimes a person was healed through touch; other times Jesus just spoke the word and the healing happened.

We see the power of the Holy Spirit in operation in Jesus' life. Jesus started His ministry after His baptism when the Holy Spirit came upon Him. Baptism is a symbol that we die to our old lives and receive the new life that Jesus offers us through His resurrection power (Romans

6:3-4). We see that Jesus didn't start His ministry until after He received the empowering power of the Holy Spirit. We also need God's Spirit to minister to people. It is not difficult; we only need to ask with a sincere heart (Matthew 7:9-11). I ask God to fill me daily. I say, "I need You, Holy Spirit; fill me, lead me, help me, change me, let me be fruitful."

When we read about the miracles, we see one amazing account after another. Listen to this one. One Sabbath Jesus was preaching in the synagogue. There was a woman whose back was bent over. She hadn't been able to straighten her back for seventeen years. The Bible says she had a spirit of infirmity. Jesus spoke to her, "Woman, you are loosed from your infirmity" (Luke 13:12b), and she was healed. What authority Jesus had! It reminds me of the way God spoke the world into being in Genesis. Each day we read, "God said," and the heavens, the earth, the plants and animals were created. Often Jesus just spoke and the person was healed.

A paralyzed man was carried on a mat and brought to Jesus. Jesus told him his sins were forgiven. The Pharisees were upset and called it blasphemy; only God could forgive sins. How could Jesus forgive this man's sins? Jesus knew what they were thinking and told them He would show them that He had the authority on earth to forgive sins. He said to the man, "Stand up, pick up your mat, and go home!" (Matthew 9:6b NLT). The man got up and went home. Can you imagine being in that crowd? They had never seen this before. They recognized that God had given Jesus great authority.

Jesus healed a man who had no hope to ever get well. The man had been paralyzed for thirty-eight years, lying at the pool of Bethesda. Many sick gathered at this pool, because on occasion an angel would stir the water and the first person who got in would be healed. This man had no one to help him to get in the pool. Can you imagine being paralyzed for thirty-eight years? That's a long time. We don't know how long he had been lying at that pool, hoping to get in. Even though people didn't help this man, God knew about him and sent Jesus to him. Jesus talked to him and asked him if he wanted to get well. The man said that he had no one to put him in the pool, and thus he could not get well. Jesus said, "Rise, take up your bed and walk" (John 5:8). The man was instantly healed. He rolled up his mat and walked. This miracle happened on the Sabbath, and the Jewish leaders were upset about Jesus healing on a Sabbath. A man who was paralyzed for thirty-eight years was healed, and they were not happy about it. Instead they bickered that it was against the Law. Jesus answered that His Father was always working and He was doing the work of His Father (John 5:17), which upset them even more. *What? God is His Father?* Even we can sometimes get stuck in a mindset and miss the will of God. Holy Spirit, help us not to be so stuck in our ways that we miss what God is doing.

Jesus was no ordinary man. Wherever He went He healed the sick, the lame, the deaf, and the blind. He revealed God's heart to those who were suffering. We do not read one account where Jesus said no, He didn't want to heal a person. We read several times where He felt compassion for the people. Jesus didn't walk around and condemn people for their sins. He knew they already knew what they were doing wrong. He told them stories—parables about who God was, about the kingdom of heaven, kingdom principles, and signs of His return. He manifested God's kingdom by healing the sick. People were amazed with the authority in His words and teaching. He offended the Pharisees but drew the crowds. Some came for the miracles; others came to hear Him preach. All along Jesus revealed the kingdom of God and God's character.

John 15 is a beautiful picture of a relationship with Jesus. It is a picture of loving and abiding. "As the Father loved Me, I also have loved you; abide in My love" (John 15:9). The Living Bible reads, "Live within my love," and The Message says, "Make yourselves at home in my love." Jesus used the picture of a vine and branches to illustrate this. He said He is the grape vine and we are the branches, and we cannot produce fruit if we are not connected to the vine. Just as the branch needs to be connected to the vine to draw sap from the vine, we need to be connected and in relationship with Jesus to produce fruit (John 15:1-3). This is a picture of a living relationship. It is not just a picture of the production of good works, but a bringing forth of good works through a relationship with Jesus. We are filled with God's Holy Spirit when we spend time with Jesus.

If we only seek the miracles and stop there, we miss so much. Jesus longs to have a relationship with us. God the Father longs to have a relationship with us. If it were not so, Jesus would have come and preached the rules—do this and do that and you will be saved. He didn't; He preached relational life. He told people He was the only way (John 14:6). The Pharisees and Sadducees were offended by what He said. They would have preferred it if Jesus had just preached the rules as they knew them, but relationship as Jesus portrayed it—God as His Father—was too much for them to receive.

Rules make people feel in control—they know what to expect. Mankind doesn't have a good track record in the area of relationships. Adam and Eve's son, Cain, killed his brother, Abel (Genesis 4). Jesus said He did not come to remove the Law, but to fulfill it (Matthew 5:17). I know and obey the rules—the Ten Commandments—not to steal, etc. I have found that Jesus is asking for a deeper commitment from me. He desires a clean heart. He died to bring us into the Hebrews 10:16 covenant "This is the covenant that I will make with them after those days, says the Lord: I will put My laws into their hearts, and in their minds I will write them." My mom and dad taught me how to behave according to biblical principles. Little things that I maybe didn't learn from them, I learned from the Bible. As I walk in relationship with God, through Jesus, in fellowship with the Holy Spirit, He helps me to walk in His ways. He convicts my heart when I do something wrong. I quickly turn and repent and get back into right relationship with Him.

There is such a blessing in walking in the fear of the Lord. If you do a word search you will find how many blessings are connected to the fear of the Lord. Some translations use the words *reverence for God* instead of *fear of the Lord*. This explains the fear of the Lord better. It does not mean being afraid of God. It means to have a heart attitude in which you honor God and have respect for God as the all-powerful King of the universe. Because I honor and respect Him, I obey Him. Then He comes and He meets me. "The secret [of the sweet, satisfying companionship] of the Lord have they who fear (revere and worship) Him, and He will show them His covenant and reveal to them its [deep, inner] meaning" (Psalm 25:14 AMP).

Miracles drew crowds to Jesus. We see miracles happen in outreach meetings in Africa. A miracle is like a candy bar or a piece of chocolate cake. It is appealing and exciting, and often the first step that draws a person into the kingdom of God. God is busy in our lives every day. We just need to look and see what He is doing around us. I heard of a family whose kids had to go out every day and come back and tell their parents where God moved that day. If they couldn't tell their parents that evening, they didn't get dessert. They developed a keen sense of noticing what God was doing in their everyday life. He wants to do something special in your life every day too. Sometimes it can be something as seemingly small as waking up with a song in our hearts. It is such a joy to see Him and walk with Him in our everyday life. If we look for Him, we will see Him!

God wants to have a personal, special relationship with each one of us. It is our choice how deep and how rich this relationship is. It starts by surrendering our lives to Him. I heard a testimony of a man who had a radical encounter with God. He was instantly set free from addictions, but God worked a process in his life to free him from rejection and performance orientation and to bring him and his family into an emotionally healthy place. John 8:32 tells us, "And you shall know the truth, and the truth shall make you free." Truth has the capacity to set us free. God knows how much we can handle and He works through a process in our lives, bringing us truth bit by bit. Deliverance can be instant; it can also be a process of renewing the mind, receiving truth, seeing dysfunctional patterns, and changing as we receive truth.

I remember how I once attended a class about rejection. I walked out of that class and said, "Phew, thank You, God; I don't have that in my life." Just about every week as I was taking the class the Holy Spirit showed me something I needed to change or repent from. The teacher of the class mentioned that perfectionism can be a sign of rejection. We had four little kids. They often made messes and I didn't get too upset about them. As I was driving home, the Holy Spirit started to talk to me. He said, "So you think you don't have rejection in your life?" I said, "I'm sure I don't have that." Then He started to show me how perfectionistic I was regarding my character—how hard I was on myself if I made the slightest mistake, felt like I said something wrong, or had done something wrong. I am thankful that He showed me that; because of it, God opened a wound that went way back in my past, one that was generational. It opened the door for healing to come.

Let us get back to the miracles. Jesus raised people from the dead. Lazarus had been dead for three days, and then Jesus showed up. Martha told Jesus that her brother wouldn't have died if Jesus had been there when he died. Jesus told her Lazarus would rise again, but she didn't understand that it was going to happen that day. Mary said the same thing, and we see how Jesus wept when He saw Mary and the others weeping at the grave. Jesus shouted, "Lazarus, come forth!" (John 11:43), and Lazarus walked out of the grave. That must have been amazing. I can imagine how astonished the people were to see Lazarus stumbling out of the tomb, all tied up in grave clothes.

One day as Jesus was walking He came across a funeral procession. They were carrying the only son of a widow. Jesus felt compassion, He touched the coffin, the funeral procession stopped, and He said, "Young man, I say to you, arise" (Luke 7:14). The young man sat up and began to speak. Look at the reaction of the people: "Then fear came upon all, and they glorified God, saying, 'A great prophet has risen up among us'; and, 'God has visited His people'" (Luke 7:16). We see in other situations too that the awe and fear of God fell upon the people when they witnessed the power of God. God revealed His power to the Israelites through the ten plagues that He sent against Egypt in the time of Moses. They didn't know Him after four hundred years of being in slavery. He continued to reveal Himself by opening the Red Sea and providing for them in the desert (Exodus 8–10).

Jesus restored a man with a deformed hand. He told him, "Stretch out your hand" (Matthew 12:13), and as the man stretched out his hand it was healed. Jesus opened the eyes of several blind people. Jesus put spittle on the eyes of the blind man of Bethsaida and the man could see, but not clearly. Jesus put His hand on his eyes again and the man could see (Mark 8:22-25). There was not one disease that was too difficult for Jesus to heal. Jesus healed the sick everywhere He went.

Jesus had dominion over nature. In Matthew 14:22-33 we read an account when Jesus sent the disciples ahead across the lake and He went up the hillside to pray. Around 3 a.m., the boat was struggling against the wind and the waves. It caused great fear when they saw a figure walking toward them on the water. Peter said with great boldness, "Lord, if it is You, command me to come to You on the water" (Matthew 14:28). Jesus told him to come. I wondered what Peter thought as he stepped out of that boat. I think at first he probably didn't think, but then as he was walking on the water and he looked at the waves his faith faltered and he began to sink. He cried out to Jesus to save him, and Jesus took his hand, and said, "O you of little faith, why did you doubt?" (Matthew 14:31). I am like that at times. When God speaks to me about a situation I have faith. For a while I have faith, but when the obstacles come I wonder, "Did I hear right? What am I missing? Am I doing something wrong?" Jesus climbed in the boat and the wind stopped. I know I want Jesus in my boat wherever I go. With Jesus by my side I have peace even if the storm rages (Philippians 4:7).

Discussion Questions: Healing the Sick

1. We have all experienced suffering and disappointment. How do you deal with a situation if you do not see immediate healing after you have prayed about it?

   _____

   _____

   _____

2. We read that Jesus felt compassion for the people, and then we read how He healed them. How important do you think is it to have compassion for people when we pray for them?

   _____

   _____

   _____

3. The prayer of faith heals the sick (James 5:15). I don't think we can say a person doesn't have enough faith when someone does not get healed, but it is important to have the revelation that Jesus not only died for our sins—He also died for our sicknesses. "By his wounds you are healed" (1 Peter 2:24 NLT, see Isaiah 53:5). Do you have faith to pray for someone who is sick? What is the reason that you think you do or do not have faith to pray for the sick?

   _____

   _____

   _____

4. Where is your focus when you pray for someone who is sick? Do you focus on the sickness, listening to the Holy Spirit, or how the person is feeling?

   _____

   _____

   _____

5. How do you respond to a situation when you don't see immediate breakthrough? Discuss how we should respond to such situations.

_____
_____
_____

6. Pondering the Word: Pick one of the following Scriptures and focus on it: 1 Peter 2:24, Isaiah 53:5, James 5:15, or Psalm 103:3. Ask God to release faith to pray for healing as you ponder these Scriptures.

Chapter 7: The Garden of Gethsemane

"He went a little farther and fell on His face, and prayed, saying, 'O My Father, if it is possible, let this cup pass from Me; nevertheless, not as I will, but as You will'" (Matthew 26:39).

Jesus went through thirty years of preparation for three years of ministry. God in His wisdom released and empowered Jesus when He was about thirty years old. I might have thought that twenty-four would have been a good age to release Jesus into ministry. It would have given Him more years of ministry. That is how my natural mind thinks, but I have learned that God knows and sees the big picture. He looks at situations in a different way. His wisdom is much higher than my wisdom (Isaiah 55:8-9).

When you climb the stairs to the top of a lighthouse, you get a different view from that of the ground. I have climbed the stairs of two different lighthouses. One was particularly high, and I could see very far. On the ground I saw the small path in front of me, and the trees or houses around me blocked my ability to see more. God sees the panoramic view. He sees the situation from above. He knows the end before the beginning (Isaiah 46:10; Psalm 139:1-4). He knows what the outcome of every choice will be even before I have made the decision.

We read how people responded to Jesus' ministry: "And so it was, when Jesus had ended these sayings, that the people were astonished at His teaching, for He taught them as one having authority, and not as the scribes" (Matthew 7:28-29). The Holy Spirit-empowered Jesus drew crowds wherever He went, but the Pharisees and Sadducees weren't happy. They were the religious leaders of the day. They felt that the people should listen to them and follow their teachings. Who was this Jesus that the crowds followed Him? They asked Jesus trick questions to see if they could find something against Him.

Jesus sent two of His disciples to go and prepare a room for the group to eat the Passover meal (Mark 14:13). Jesus knew He was going to leave this earth soon. He told the disciples that He had to go to Jerusalem, He would suffer many terrible things by the hands of the religious leaders, and He would be killed and raised again on the third day. Peter took Jesus aside and told Him this would not happen to Him. Jesus rebuked Peter and said he was seeing things from man's perspective, not from God's perspective (Mark 8:32-33). The shock and terror when those things unfolded was so tremendous that the disciples scattered and Peter denied Jesus. There was nothing that could prepare the disciples for the horror of what happened when their dearest friend and teacher walked through His final days and hours on earth.

What would you do if you knew you had little time left with someone? Jesus acted much differently than I would have expected. I would think, "Now is the time to make the best, most encouraging speech I can." Jesus got up from the table, took a towel, filled a basin with water, and washed the disciples' feet! We see how Peter responded: "'You shall never wash my feet!' Jesus answered him, 'If I do not wash you, you have no part with Me'" (John 13:8). How quickly Peter changed his mind and told Jesus, "Don't just wash my feet, but my hands and my head, too." I can't help but smile at Peter's reaction. I probably would have said the same thing. The disciples and those who followed Jesus interpreted what Jesus said and did in the natural and often missed what Jesus was really saying. *He will give me living water—where is His bucket? You will tear down the temple and rebuild it in three days—it is not possible.* Jesus spoke in parables and metaphors. He spoke truth from a heavenly perspective. The disciples didn't understand what He said and asked Jesus when they were alone what the parables meant. That is how we are when we look at a situation in the natural and feel we do not know what to do or what is the right decision to make. When the

Holy Spirit brings revelation or insight, it is like a light bulb gets turned on and we suddenly know what we should do.

Jesus humbled Himself by kneeling before each disciple and washing their feet. During His last hours with His disciples, He gave them an example of humility and serving one another: "If I then, your Lord and Teacher, have washed your feet, you also ought to wash one another's feet" (John 13:14). Their love for one another would prove to the world that they were His disciples.

Jesus came to earth in humility. He wasn't born in a palace. He lived an ordinary life until the Holy Spirit empowered Him. Philippians 2 reveals to us why God has exalted Him to the highest place in the universe.

> "You must have the same attitude that Christ Jesus had. Though he was God, he did not think of equality with God as something to cling to. Instead, he gave up his divine privileges; he took the humble position of a slave and was born as a human being. When he appeared in human form, he humbled himself in obedience to God and died a criminal's death on a cross" (Philippians 2:5-8 NLT).

God exalted Jesus and gave Him the highest honor and a name with more authority than any other name, because Jesus humbled Himself. Verse 9 tells us that every knee in heaven and on the earth and under the earth will bow to the name of Jesus. There is no power or authority higher than the name of Jesus (Philippians 2:9-11). If a person does not bow to Him while living on earth, then in eternity there will be no choice. Everyone will bow before Jesus.

The disciples came to Jesus and asked Him where He wanted them to prepare the Passover meal that evening. Jesus gave them specific instructions, saying when they entered Jerusalem they would see a man carrying a pitcher of water. They were to follow him to the house where he was going and ask the owner of the house if Jesus and His disciples could have their Passover meal there. Jesus said the man would take them upstairs to a guest room that was already set up and they should prepare the meal there. It all happened just like Jesus said (Mark 14:12-16). Jesus received all this information by revelation from God. What an exact word of knowledge! During the Passover meal, Jesus directed them in a new way. "And as they were eating, Jesus took bread, blessed and broke it, and gave it to them and said, "Take, eat; this is My body." Then He took the cup, and when He had given thanks He gave it to them, and they all drank from it. And He said to them, "This is My blood of the new covenant, which is shed for many" (Mark 14:22-24). What a surprising Passover this must have been.

Jesus instructed His disciples to remember Him this way. The bread and the wine (or grape juice) confirms the covenant between God and His people. He told them to do this in remembrance of Him. When we take Communion, we remember what Jesus has done for us on the cross (1 Corinthians 11:23-26). Around this dinner table, Jesus revealed that Peter would deny Him and Judas was planning to betray Him.

During His last days with the disciples, Jesus shared so much with them. Most of it they didn't understand. Jesus told them He would leave and prepare a place for them in heaven and then He would come back and get them. Thomas said that they had no idea where this place was. Jesus spoke about spiritual things, and Thomas tried to understand them literally. Jesus continued, "I am the way, the truth, and the life. No one comes to the Father except through Me" (John 14:6). Philip responded and asked that Jesus would show them the Father. Jesus said that anyone who had seen Him had seen the Father (John 14:8-10).

Jesus shared with them that He would ask His Father to give them another Comforter, the Holy Spirit, who would not leave them and would lead them in the truth. Many of the things Jesus told them they didn't understand at first, but if we look at the disciples in Acts, we notice their responses have changed. When they heard someone was following Jesus they asked the person, "Did you receive the Holy Spirit?" Eventually they understood the things Jesus had been saying. Jesus told them He would come back to life, and those who obeyed Him were the ones who loved Him and He would reveal Himself to them. Here Judas (not Judas Iscariot) asked Jesus why He would only reveal Himself to them and not to the world. Jesus answered that He revealed Himself to those who obeyed and loved Him (John 14:15-24). This reminds me of the Scripture that says God "is a rewarder of those who diligently seek Him" (Hebrews 11:6). Just as we at times can have an experience or encounter with the Holy Spirit, the Christian life is a diligent pursuit of God. We cannot just emphasize the encounter or just emphasize the discipline. God has a unique journey for each of us. It looks different from everyone else's journey. Only you can live your life and discover your journey. It is worth it to pursue God diligently and to pursue Him with your whole heart and go on this journey with Him.

John 15 is a key chapter with a secret to the Christian life. Jesus said He is the vine and His Father is the gardener who tends this vine. Those who love Jesus are the branches on the vine. A branch needs sap from the vine to stay alive. We need to be connected to Jesus and go to Him often to receive spiritual life (John 15:1-9). When I spend time listening to worship music, I sometimes feel how the joy and peace of Jesus fills me. We can receive His life when we spend time with Him in prayer, read our Bibles, focus on a Scripture, or even just sit still focusing on Jesus. The secret is to abide, remain, or to live in Him and allow Him to live in us—to make room for Him in our lives. During your day, just turn your thoughts to Jesus and talk to Him through short prayers. *Thank You, Jesus, that You're here with me; help me with this task; I release this concern to You,* etc. Jesus modeled a lifestyle of dependence and trust in His Father, spending time in the evenings in prayer with His Father. How much more do we need to live in dependence upon Him.

In John 17 Jesus poured out His heart in prayer to His Father, "Father, the hour has come. Glorify Your Son, that Your Son also may glorify You, as You have given Him authority over all flesh, that He should give eternal life to as many as You have given Him. And this is eternal life, that they may know You, the only true God, and Jesus Christ whom You have sent" (John 17:1-3). With my natural eyes I can see no glory in Jesus going to the cross. I had difficulty understanding Hebrews 12:2 that talks about Jesus, "who for the joy that was set before Him endured the cross." What possible joy could there be in dying on a cross? Then the Holy Spirit reminded me of when my children were born. I had long painful labors, but when the babies were born I soon forgot the pain. The joy of a new life causes a mother to quickly forget the pain and the suffering. The joy of giving people eternal life outweighed the suffering and pain that Jesus endured on the cross. Jesus went to the cross seeing you and I and every person who has ever lived and who will ever be born. The joy of what He would receive—a people restored in relationship with God—made the pain and suffering He endured worth it.

Jesus prayed for those who believed in Him and those who would come to believe in Him. He asked God to protect and keep them safe. He asked God that they would be one with Him, just as He and His Father are one. How do we accomplish oneness with Jesus? In my walk with Jesus, there have been times when I felt close to Him and other times when He felt far away. I have learned to walk in the truth that He is with me wherever I go. He is as close as my next breath, whether I feel Him or not—even when I am not aware of His presence with me (Psalm 139:1-4). I learned to walk by faith and not by what I feel. I love the times when I am more aware of His presence. During difficult times—for example, when my mother was critically ill in the hospital—I often checked how I felt in my heart/spirit. At times, in the most challenging situations, I had peace; other times there was a burden in my spirit and I knew I had to pray. God brought me through those five weeks when my mom was in the ICU, and she couldn't talk and respond, with His strength. To me this is a small glimpse of oneness with Jesus—feeling His heart in situations and responding accordingly.

Listening to worship music can draw us into God's presence. When I was in South Africa, I did not have any worship music with me; I often found God's presence early in the morning when the sun was coming up, looking out the French doors of my mom's apartment, watching the geese, ducks, chickens and other animals wake up. In those moments the Holy Spirit ministered peace to my heart. I positioned my heart to hear Him. Most days I didn't hear a whole lot. I thought maybe I would see a vision or hear Him say something, but most of the time I just sensed His peace. Other days I remembered a song, read Scripture, or I saw a picture which was a message of what He was saying. Sometimes I found Jesus in silence, other times in prayer or Scripture; often I found Him in nature. There were things I didn't understand and answers that He didn't give, but I learned to trust Him during that difficult time, moment by moment, day by day.

Jesus was entering the most difficult time of His earthly life and ministry. Soon He would be betrayed by a friend—a disciple who had walked with Him and helped Him for three years. Judas could be bought, and he betrayed Jesus. What did Jesus do in preparation for this difficult time? He went to the garden and spent time in prayer. He agonized about what was to come—such agony that His sweat turned into drops of blood. He asked God if this cup could be removed from Him. Was it really necessary that the Son of God, the God who created the universe, the One who has unlimited power available to Him, should have to die? Was there no other way? God had put the requirements in place. The shedding of blood was the only thing that could cover sin (Leviticus 17:11; Hebrews 9:22). For about two thousand years the Israelites brought bulls and goats as sacrifices to cover their sins. "The sacrifices under that system were repeated again and again, year after year, but they were never able to provide perfect cleansing for those who came to worship" (Hebrews 10:1b NLT). These animals had to be perfect, without blemish, pointing to the One to come, the One who would bring the complete sacrifice for sins. "But our High Priest offered himself to God as a single sacrifice for sins, good for all time" (Hebrews 10:12 NLT).

There was and will be only one perfect man in history, and this is Jesus Christ. He was the only One who could be a perfect sacrifice for sins. God required of Him to lay down His life. Jesus could have called millions of angels to come to His rescue in the garden of Gethsemane when they came for Him (Matthew 26:53). He had to willingly lay down His life and allow men to treat Him in this cruel and horrible way.

Judas and the priests and elders came armed with swords and sticks. Judas greeted Jesus with a kiss. Jesus said, "My friend, go ahead and do what you have come for" (Matthew 26:50 NLT). Simon Peter, one of Jesus' disciples, drew his sword and cut off the high priest's servant's ear. Even here we see Jesus act with compassion, as He healed the man's ear. Then His disciples became fearful and fled. Jesus was alone, facing those who accused Him.

They took Him to Annas, who was Israel's high priest (A.D. 6-15). Annas was deposed by the Romans, and his son-in-law Caiaphas appointed as a high priest (A.D. 18-36/37). Jesus first faced the high priest, Annas. He asked Jesus about His teaching. Then Jesus was sent to Caiaphas (John 18:12-24). The priests were trying to find witnesses to accuse Jesus. Jesus remained silent when He was accused. The only time He spoke was when He was asked if He was the Son of God. "You have said it. And in the future you will see the Son of Man seated in the place of power at God's right hand and coming on the clouds of heaven" (Matthew 26:64 NLT). Jesus had no identity crisis. He knew who He was.

Meanwhile Peter was waiting outside in the courtyard. His wonderful, kindhearted Rabbi was beginning the journey that would take Him to the cross. A servant girl recognized Peter and told him that he was one of those who walked with Jesus. Peter denied it in front of everyone. A second time and third time he said, "I do not know the Man!" (Matthew 26:72). The rooster crowed. Suddenly, Jesus' words came back to him, "Before the rooster crows, you will deny Me three times" (Matthew 26:75). Peter left, weeping bitterly. Peter was heartbroken. Jesus had warned him and still he had denied Him. The fear of man, fear of being ridiculed, or fear of being rejected can keep us silent when we need to speak up. That is why we need the Holy Spirit. The disciples weren't bold until the Holy Spirit empowered them. We need power from on high!

Hermie Reynolds

Discussion Questions: The Garden of Gethsemane

1. Seeing Jesus being captured was a fearful situation for the disciples. How do you respond in situations which stir fear in your heart?

2. Discuss different ways people respond when they are falsely accused. How would you respond? What is the right response?

3. Peter denied that he knew Jesus when Jesus was taken to the religious leaders. Would you have the courage to take a stand for your faith if you were tested in such a way? What could you do to strengthen your faith?

4. Read Isaiah 55:8-9. Think about a time when a situation didn't turn out the way you thought it would. When the enemy is at work, God allows even the bad situations to work for our good. Read Romans 8:28. Give opportunity for a few people to share in short what happened and what they learned in situations like this.

5. Jesus said if He left the earth God would send the Holy Spirit. He also gave us the picture of the vine and branches (John 15). Share any valuable insight that you have learned about living in relationship with Jesus.

_____
_____
_____
_____

6. Pondering the Word: Choose a verse or phrase from John 15:1-10 and focus on it. Write down any insights or thoughts that you have about this section of Scripture.

_____
_____
_____
_____
_____
_____

Chapter 8: The Cross

> "After saying all these things, Jesus looked up to heaven and said, 'Father the hour has come. Glorify your Son so he can give glory back to you'" (John 17:1 NLT).

Jesus didn't defend Himself or His teachings. When the elders and priests made their accusations, Jesus remained silent (Matthew 27:11-14). The religious leaders sent Him to Pilate, the Roman governor. The only question He answered was about His identity. Pilate asked Him if He was the King of the Jews. Jesus answered, "You have said it" (Matthew 27:11 NLT). Pilate heard Jesus was a Galilean and realized Jesus was under Herod's jurisdiction. Herod had heard about Jesus and wanted to see Jesus do a miracle, but Jesus didn't live up to his expectations. He didn't do any miracles and didn't respond to the questions Herod asked Him. Herod and the soldiers began to mock Jesus. They put a royal robe around Him and sent Him back to Pilate (Luke 23:8-12). In the midst of accusations, Jesus did not defend Himself (John 18:28-38).

In answer to Pilate's question if He was the king of the Jews, Jesus responded that His kingdom was not an earthly kingdom. "I was born and came into the world to testify to the truth. All who love the truth recognize that what I say is true" (John 18:37 NLT). Pilate went out to where the crowd was waiting. He said, "He is not guilty of any crime" (John 18:38 NLT). During the Passover celebration, Pilate had the opportunity to release a criminal. He asked the crowd whether they wanted Barabbas, a murderer, to be released, or if he should release Jesus. The crowd demanded that Barabbas should be released, and when Pilate asked them what he should do with Jesus they kept on yelling, "Crucify Him!" I can feel my spirit cringe on the inside when I read those words—*crucify Him*. How hard must their hearts have been to want to crucify an innocent man who healed so many people. Pilate released Barabbas and handed Jesus over to be whipped and crucified (John 19:1-16). If we open our hearts to seek the truth, we will find the truth about who Jesus was and still is. I can see why Jesus said that to enter the kingdom of God we should be like children (Matthew 18:3).

Jesus stepped out of eternity, was born as a baby in a human body, and lived and walked on the earth to show us God the Father's nature. He knew His purpose—to make His Father known and to walk and live in obedience to His Father. Jesus told Pilate He was a King and His kingdom was not from this earth. Pilate had no authority over Him if God didn't give it to him (John 19:11). Jesus had no identity crisis; He knew why He was on the earth. He knew what He had to do. His mind was set on what He was going to accomplish in the spirit realm. He was going to overcome the spiritual powers and principalities through His death and set free all those who would receive this free gift of salvation and deliverance offered to them through His sacrifice on the cross (Colossians 2:15).

Jesus chose to lay down His life. If His Father had not allowed it, no one would have been able to touch Him. Willingly the King of Kings went to the cross. Willingly He submitted to the whipping, the mocking, and the crown of thorns on His head. Willingly He endured…because He saw you and He saw me!

Our oldest son went to Bible school after he finished high school. As part of the Bible school training, the students had to spend a certain amount of time in God's presence in the prayer room each week. He had been seeking God the first semester and wasn't feeling that he was accomplishing much. After Christmas break when he went back, he had an encounter with Jesus. He was sitting in the prayer room with his eyes closed, talking to Jesus. Then he felt somebody touch his arm and sit down next to him. He opened his eyes and saw nobody there. In his spirit he knew it was Jesus who sat down next to him. He started to ask the Lord questions in his mind and heard Jesus answer him in his mind. He asked Jesus why He went to the cross. Jesus showed him the people standing around the cross as He was crucified, and He said, "I did it for them." He showed him people from all through the ages and said, "I did it for them." Then my son saw himself standing there amongst the crowd at the cross and Jesus said, "I did it for you!" When we seek God, we will find Him, and we find Him through His Son, Jesus. "He came to his own people, and even they rejected him. But to all who believed him and accepted him, he gave the right to become children of God" (John 1:11-12 NLT).

There He was—Jesus was facing His biggest trial in His life. He was going to take the sin of the world upon Himself—all the sin and wrongdoing of everyone who used to live, everyone who is living today, and all the people who will ever live on the earth. That is a big load! An animal could cover sins for a time, but then the sacrifice would have to be repeated. Jesus, the perfect God-man, was the only One who could be a one-time sacrifice—and then no more sacrifices would be needed. Jesus stepped into our place and took the wrath of God against all ungodliness and unrighteousness (Romans 1:18). "He who believes in the Son has everlasting life; and he who does not believe the Son shall not see life, but the wrath of God abides on him" (John 3:36).

Three times Pilate said Jesus was not guilty. The crowd continued to demand that He should be crucified. Pilate washed his hands in a bowl and told the people he was innocent in killing Jesus. The blood of Jesus would be upon them and their families. Pilate released Barabbas and ordered Jesus to be whipped with a lead-tipped whip. Jesus was released to the Roman soldiers. They put a crown of thorns on His head, a scarlet robe around Him, and gave Him a stick for a scepter in His hand. They mocked Him, spit on Him, grabbed the stick, and hit Him with it while mocking and taunting Him (Matthew 27:24-31).

After he listened to an account of the cross, a young boy made this comment, "Jesus shouldn't have come." Looking at the suffering that Jesus endured we would think, *How could anyone willingly go through that kind of suffering?* Jesus saw the bigger picture. He looked at the end result of what the cross would accomplish—freedom from sin, relationship with God, restoration, healing, deliverance, sons and daughters of God who could walk in the anointing of the Holy Spirit.

"I tell you the truth, anyone who believes in me will do the same works I have done, and even greater works, because I am going to be with the Father" (John 14:12 NLT). Jesus trained disciples, and the disciples received the mandate to train disciples. That mandate is still being completed; disciples of Jesus are still being trained and released to train more disciples. Receiving Jesus as Savior is just the beginning. We can't stop there. Every believer is called to impact the area and people where they live. We can love those around us, pray for needs, and pray for those who are sick. We can make a difference wherever we go. Many people have been stuck in problems that hinder them from seeing beyond themselves. We are not born as adults and we don't come into the kingdom of God as mature Christians. Just as we grow physically, we need to grow and mature spiritually too. We grow from being children, where everything is about what we can get, to loving Jesus and shifting our focus to how we can help.

Jesus carried His cross, beaten and bruised, physically not strong enough for such a task. On the way the soldiers commanded Simon from Cyrene to carry Jesus' cross (Matthew 27:32). A huge crowd and many weeping woman followed Jesus to Golgotha. They arrived at Golgotha, and the soldiers nailed Jesus to the cross. Casting lots they determined how to divide His clothes between them (Mark 15:24). A sign with the criminal's name and his crime was usually written on a board and hung around his neck. A sign was nailed to the cross above Jesus' head, "Jesus of Nazareth, the King of the Jews" (John 19:19). It was meant to be a mockery, but the truth was that Jesus through His death was actually coming into His kingdom. His death would bring freedom and salvation to millions of people.

The soldiers offered Jesus wine mixed with gall to drink. Jesus refused it (Mark 15:23). Two criminals were crucified with Jesus, one on each side (Luke 23:33). One of the criminals insulted Jesus and told Him if He was the Messiah He should save Himself. The other criminal rebuked him and said, "Don't you fear God even when you have been sentenced to die? We deserve to die for our crimes, but this man hasn't done anything wrong" (Luke 23:40-41 NLT). Jesus recognized this man's faith and told him that day he would be in paradise with Him

(Luke 23:32-43). Here was a criminal who was sentenced to die, and Jesus saved his soul during the last few hours of his earthly life. This man had no time to do good deeds or make restitution for the wrong he did. Yes, there was a better, more fruitful and fulfilling way of life that he could have lived if he had made better choices, yet Jesus saw his faith and saved his soul. This is the grace of God. Jesus saves! "And this is the way to have eternal life—to know you, the only true God, and Jesus Christ, the one you sent to earth" (John 17:3 NLT).

Jesus, an innocent man, was nailed to a cross to die a criminal's death. What did Jesus do? He forgave them: "Father, forgive them, for they do not know what they do" (Luke 23:34). I don't think you can go through life without experiencing a situation where you have to forgive someone. We live on a fallen earth where people hurt each other; they are impatient, misunderstandings happen, and we will get hurt. To forgive those who hurt us is a lesson best learned quickly. If it is hard to forgive; I ask Jesus to help me to forgive.

Even on the cross Jesus was concerned about those He loved. He saw His mother, Mary, standing near the cross and told John to take care of His mother. From then on John took Mary into his home. This is God's heart. He places the lonely into families (Psalm 68:6). Jesus called out, "My God, my God, why have You forsaken Me?" (Matthew 27:46). Jesus, who walked and lived in close fellowship with His Dad doing only what He saw His Father doing, was going through the biggest trial of His life. The triune God—Father, Son, and Holy Spirit—had never been separated throughout all eternity. This must have been even more painful than the physical pain, to feel abandoned by God the Father. Jesus obeyed; He became the Mediator between God and mankind; He became the sacrifice, received the wrath for sin, and experienced separation from God. He did it to open the way so that you and I could be restored in fellowship with God.

Jesus' words, "I am thirsty" (John 19:28 NLT) reveal His humanity (John 19:30). Wine mixed with gall was given to Him. He was fully human, God in the flesh. He did not use any supernatural power to not feel the pain. He experienced all the physical pain any person would experience dying such a horrible death.

Then He spoke His last words: "It is finished!" (John 19:30) and "Father, into Your hands I commit My spirit" (Luke 23:46) and breathed His last breath. He had completed His assignment. He came to earth to give His life that we could have life. The Bible tells us that there is no greater love than when one person gives his life for another. Jesus gave the ultimate sacrifice. He gave His life. He stepped into your place and my place and said, *Father, forgive them, for they don't know what they are doing. Father, here is the sacrifice on their behalf. I pay the price so that they can go free.*

Even nature could not witness Jesus taking the sin of the world upon Him. Darkness settled over the land from noon to three in the afternoon. Psalm 19 compares the sun to a radiant bridegroom. When Jesus, our radiant bridegroom, died, the earth trembled and the sun hid its face. Jesus, the One who holds creation together (Colossians 1:17), became a substitute for all mankind's sin, ungodliness, and unrighteousness. He died for all people throughout time.

My relationship with Jesus and my love for Him keeps me from sinning. I know it hurts His heart and it hurts my relationship with Him when I sin. Loving God more than sin keeps me from sinning. We don't need to walk in sin consciousness. I can see why the Bible tells us to focus on what is good and lovely and pursue peace. Where our focus is, that is the place we will walk. I think the most challenging area for me is my heart attitude; sometimes I get impatient with my family or find a negative or critical thought in my heart that I need to take to the cross. Our close relationships are the most challenging. After so many years of walking with Jesus and allowing the Holy Spirit to cleanse my heart and life, my anchor has moved from insecurity and fear to be anchored in Jesus' love for me and what He has done on the cross. My trust is in His ability. My faith is in Him—on the days that I feel His presence and during the times when it feels like life is falling apart. I run to Him, ask for His help and continue to ask for His help, and He brings me through every situation.

I cannot imagine the agony and pain that Jesus went through dying such a horrible death on the cross. Being the Son of God, Jesus did not cry out and say, "God, save me from this," or "Father, send legions of angels to rescue Me." Can you imagine what it was like in the spirit realm as angels and demons watched Jesus die? We know that the demons knew who He was. Several times Jesus quieted demons when they manifested when He came near Him (Matthew 8:29). He was tempted by the Devil in the desert. Satan and his demons knew who was being crucified. The angels were being held back by God's orders. The One they served and worshiped was being crucified by men!

We see three supernatural events happen at this time—darkness for three hours, the earth shaking as Jesus died, and the veil in the temple tearing from top to bottom at the same time (Matthew 27:51). The veil separated the inner sanctuary, the Holy of Holies, from the Holy Place where the priests did their duties. It separated people from God's presence. The high priest was allowed to go into that room once a year on the Day of Atonement, and none of the other priests or people could enter there. God did meet with Moses there, but we do not read of others who were allowed to enter that room (Exodus 25:22). God tore that veil when Jesus died; the separation between God and man was no longer needed. "We can boldly enter heaven's Most Holy Place because of the blood of Jesus. By his death, Jesus opened a new and life-giving way through the curtain into the Most Holy Place" (Hebrews 10:19-20 NLT).

The earth shook, rocks split apart, and the bodies of many godly men and women were raised from the dead. They appeared to people in the city after Jesus was resurrected. We see the response of the Roman soldiers: "Truly this was the Son of God!" (Matthew 27:54). They had mocked Jesus before He was crucified; now they had changed their minds. Joseph from Arimathea asked Pilate for Jesus' body. It was released to him and he wrapped it in cloth and buried it in a cave-like tomb with a big rock to close the entrance to the grave (Matthew 27:57-60).

This was an intense time in history. Wherever Jesus went people were stirred, some with awe about the miracles, others with the way He was teaching. There was something different about this man. His reputation spread farther than Jerusalem. The religious leaders thought that everything would end with Jesus' death; instead, His kingdom grew and today includes people from every nation, tongue, and tribe.

> "But God has opened the eyes of those called to salvation, both Jews and Gentiles, to see that Christ is the mighty power of God to save them; Christ himself is the center of God's wise plan for their salvation. This so-called 'foolish' plan of God is far wiser than the wisest plan of the wisest man, and God in his weakness—Christ dying on the cross—is far stronger than any man" (1 Corinthians 1:24-25 TLB).

Hermie Reynolds

Discussion Questions: The Cross

1. The religious leaders of Jesus' time felt such an intense hatred against Him that they chose to release a convicted murderer instead of Jesus who was innocent. If you ever found yourself in a situation in which you were persecuted for your faith, what would your reaction be?

2. How real is the cross to you? Can you believe Jesus died *for you*? Can you believe that if you were the only person on earth He still would have done what He did—just for you? If it is difficult for you to believe this, why do you think that is? One reason could be that we don't value ourselves the way God values us. Write down your thoughts around this.

3. Jesus endured the cross, the pain, the mocking, even though He could have just whispered to His Father to end it all. Jesus had a different focus. How does our focus help us endure through difficult times?

4. Jesus said, "It is finished!" (John 19:30). The work Jesus did on the cross is finished. He died for every sin that has been committed and will be committed. We receive His forgiveness through grace. How do we walk in this amazing grace and yet not keep on sinning because that grace is available?

_____
_____
_____

5. If you were at the cross and you saw the darkness for three hours, the earthquake, heard that the veil in the temple had been torn from top to bottom—do you think you would have been convinced that something supernatural had happened?

_____
_____
_____
_____

6. Pondering the Word: Colossians 1:20-22, Philippians 2:8-11, Hebrews 12:2, 1 Corinthians 1:24-25. Choose one of the Scriptures to focus on. Write down thoughts that come to you. What is the Holy Spirit ministering to you from the passage you chose?

_____
_____
_____
_____
_____
_____
_____
_____

Chapter 9: The Blood of Jesus

> "And he said to them, 'This is my blood, which confirms the covenant between God and his people. It is poured out as a sacrifice for many'" (Mark 14:24 NLT).

Somewhere in the mystery of God breathing life into the clay figure, Adam, a miracle happened. Blood started to flow in Adam's veins, and a living, functioning body came into being. The book of Leviticus reveals to us, "For the life of the flesh is in the blood" (Leviticus 17:11). Life is in the blood? Yes, without blood in our bodies, we cannot stay alive. More than forty percent of blood loss will result in death, and the human spirit and soul leaving the body and entering into eternity.

The rest of Leviticus 17:11 reveals the importance of blood: "For the life of the flesh is in the blood, and I have given it to you upon the altar to make atonement for your souls; for it is the blood that makes atonement for the soul." God required a life for the atonement or covering of sins or ungodliness—the ways we fall short of being perfect like God. It is impossible to be 100 percent perfect like God. The Ten Commandments start with, "You shall have no other gods before Me" (Exodus 20:3). Who has never given anything a higher priority than God? Who has never had a negative or judgmental thought against someone else? The Ten Commandments show us that we cannot obey God's law 100 percent. "For no one can ever be made right with God by doing what the law commands. The law simply shows us how sinful we are" (Romans 3:20 NLT). One came who died in our place and He obeyed the law 100 percent.

If we lived on an island it might be easier not to sin. If you have people in your life, they will make you angry, annoy you, etc. We need to be cleansed of the ways we fall short of being like Jesus. I remember how I regularly sat down with my kids and told them, "Do you think you are angry at your sister and judged her because she is so bossy?" Then to our daughter, "Do you think you are mad at your brother because he doesn't want to listen to you?" There was a time when I had to do this every three weeks. They asked Jesus for forgiveness for judging and being mad at each other. Then they forgave each other, the slate was clean and all was well for a while—until the resentment escalated again. I can see this has produced good fruit. They all get along very well as young adults. They love each other and make room for each other when they can find time in their busy schedules.

God told Noah not to eat meat with blood in it (Genesis 9:4). He gave the same command to the Israelites (Deuteronomy 12:23). The blood of animals had huge significance for the Israelites in the Bible. When God delivered them from Egypt, He gave them special instructions the night before the tenth plague. Each family had to take a one-year-old male lamb without blemish, and kill it. They had to roast the meat and eat it that evening. The blood of the lamb had to be smeared on the doorposts and lintels of their houses. The blood would be a sign for the angel of death to pass by their house. The firstborn children and animals of the families in Egypt died, but the Israelite families were protected. God gave them instructions to remember this event yearly as the Passover (Exodus 12:1-25).

God freed the Israelites from the Egyptians. In the desert on their way to the Promised Land, He gave Moses instructions to build the tabernacle—a huge tent overlaid with badger's skins (Exodus 36:8-38). The tabernacle had a fence around it and a gate to the east (Exodus 38:9-31). In the outside courtyard there was a huge bronze washbasin where the priests washed their hands (Exodus 38:8; 40:1-8). There was also an altar where the priests brought many offerings or sacrifices to God. The burnt offering was for sin in general, and a male animal—a cow, sheep, goat, pigeon, or turtledove—could be brought as a sacrifice for sin (Leviticus 1:2-4). The people of Israel brought the grain offering as a gift of thankfulness for God's provision. This offering was seasoned with salt, a precious commodity in ancient times. The salt reminded them of God's covenant, or promises to them (Leviticus 2:1-16). The peace offering was an offering made to express gratitude, and a way to maintain relationship with God (Leviticus 3:1-17). The sin offering was brought as a payment for sins committed unintentionally against God and others (Leviticus 4:2). The person bringing the offering was expected to come willing to repent and confess their sins. Without repentance there was no purpose in bringing the offering.

Part of the daily sacrifices was to offer a year old lamb in the morning and evening (Exodus 29:38-39). "These burnt offerings are to be made each day from generation to generation. Offer them in the Lord's presence at the Tabernacle entrance; there I will meet with you and speak with you" (Exodus 29:42 NLT). Twice a day a lamb was sacrificed. Just pause a second and imagine this. Twice a day the Israelites saw this picture—day after day, a lamb needed to be sacrificed so they would be able to come into the place where God could speak to them. The picture shouted *a lamb is needed, a lamb is needed*—over and over. Jesus died at the time when the lambs for the Passover meal were being killed. A Lamb was needed at the exact time Jesus was crucified. Revelation 13:8 reveals Jesus is "the Lamb slain from the foundation of the world." Before God created the world, He knew a Lamb would be needed. The only Lamb who could once and forever take care of sin was His Son, the Lamb of God.

The tabernacle was divided into two rooms—the Holy Place and the Holy of Holies. The Holy Place contained the table of showbread, the lampstand, and the altar of incense. The two rooms were separated with a curtain, called the veil (Exodus 40:21). This curtain separated God's presence from the priests and the people. They were not allowed to enter that place. Inside this inner sanctuary was the ark of the covenant. It was a wooden box made from acacia wood, about 3¾ feet long, 2¼ feet wide, and 2¼ feet high, overlaid inside and out with gold. The lid of this box was made from pure gold. It was called the mercy seat. Two angels made from beaten gold were placed on each end facing each other. Their wings were spread over the mercy seat (Exodus 25:17-22). Inside the ark were the two stone tablets with the Ten Commandments written on them (Exodus 25:10-21), Aaron's rod that budded (Numbers 17:1-11), and a golden pot with manna (Hebrews 9:4). God told Moses that from above the mercy seat He would speak to him about the people of Israel (Exodus 25:22). The earthly tabernacle was only a copy, a shadow, a picture of what was to come.

The priests entered the Holy Place to do their duties. They had to fill the lampstand with oil to keep it burning (Exodus 37:17-28), change the bread on the table (Exodus 37:10-16), and keep the incense altar burning (Exodus 37:25-29). "The priests regularly entered the first room as they performed their religious duties. But only the high priest ever entered the Most Holy Place, and only once a year. And he always offered blood for his own sins and for the sin the people had committed in ignorance" (Hebrews 9:6-7 NLT). Even when the high priest went into that inner room, if he disobeyed God and did not follow the instructions exactly, he would die. God is holy, and no man or woman could approach God and go into that inner sanctuary; the holiness of God would kill them. If you think about earthly kings, few people can even get an appointment to speak to a king. In the book of Esther, we read how Esther risked her life when she walked uninvited into the king's presence (Esther 4:11). If the king extended his scepter to her she would live; if he didn't, she would be killed. If it is impossible to get the ear of an earthly king or president, how then can we enter into the presence of God, the King and Creator of the universe?

Those who were not part of the priesthood could go into the outer courtyard to bring a sacrifice. Only the priests were allowed in the Holy Place to do their duties. The high priest was allowed to come into God's presence in the inner room, the Holy of Holies, and only once a year. If I had lived during those days, I probably would have thought that it was impossible to get close to God. If even the high priest was not good enough to go into the Holy of Holies at any time, I would have no chance. The truth is, I have no chance of entering God's presence outside of Jesus, the perfect sacrificial Lamb of God.

On the Day of Atonement, the high priest had to bring a bull as an offering for his own sins and those of his family. Then, after he cleansed himself the way God required, he went into the Holy of Holies with the blood of the bull and sprinkled it on the east side of the mercy seat and then seven times in front of it. The people brought the high priest two male goats. One was sacrificed for the sin of the people, and the other driven into the wilderness. This was determined by the casting of lots (in modern times it can be compared to the rolling of dice). He sprinkled the blood of the goat in the Holy of Holies the same way as he did with the blood of the bull. Then he went outside and placed his hands upon the head of the living goat. He confessed the sin of the people of Israel over it. A man was appointed to lead the goat into a place in the wilderness where the goat would not be able to return. This goat would carry the sin of the people to a place where it could not be found (Leviticus 16). This was repeated year after year on the Day of Atonement. It reminds me of Psalm 103:12, "He has removed our sins as far from us as the east is from the west" (NLT).

The Day of Atonement was the most important holy day on the Hebrew calendar. It was a day set aside for God, a day of repentance. Nobody was allowed to work (Leviticus 23:26-32). It was the day that the high priest went into the Holy of Holies to sprinkle blood on the mercy seat of the ark of the covenant. It was the day that the nation would find out if the blood of the bull and goat was sufficient to cover their sin and rebellion, whether God would forgive them and receive them. The high priest entering the Holy of Holies on the Day of Atonement was a picture of a better system to come. We read about this better system in Hebrews 9 and 10. After He was resurrected, Jesus "entered that greater, more perfect Tabernacle in heaven, which was not made by human hands and is not part of this created world. With his own blood—not the blood of goats and calves—he entered the Most Holy Place once for all time and secured our redemption forever" (Hebrews 9:11-12 NLT). Think about those words, "secured our redemption forever." There is nothing in this world that can provide 100 percent security. I am so thankful that Jesus secured our salvation and it is not dependent on how well we perform. We can rest in walking with the Holy Spirit, trusting that He is working in our lives and knowing He will show us when we get off track.

This is a picture of where we would be without the blood of Jesus. God is completely holy. Sin or compromise cannot come into His presence. They were afraid the high priest would die when he entered the Holy of Holies to go into the presence of God. That is where we are without the blood of Jesus. Without the blood of Jesus we are not good enough, we cannot approach God, we cannot enter into His presence, our prayers are not heard. Thank You, Jesus, that Your blood is sprinkled on the mercy seat for us in heaven. The mercy seat cries, *mercy, mercy, mercy*, not because of what we have done, but because of the sacrifice of Jesus. We humble ourselves, ask for His forgiveness, and receive His mercy. He forgives, accepts, and receives us.

The curtain or veil between the Holy Place and Holy of Holies supernaturally ripped from top to bottom when Jesus died. What did that veil tell the people? The message was that once a year only the high priest was good enough to come into God's presence. That veil ripped. It screamed a message. The separation was gone! The price had been paid! Jesus opened the way! The ultimate sacrifice is paid! *You* can come into God's presence! Anyone who has a desire to come into God's presence can receive this sacrifice of the Lamb and be made righteous, be made good enough—because of what Jesus has done!

If I ask a Christian, "What did the sacrifice of Jesus do for you?" I am sure the answer I will receive is, "He died for my sins." That is true. Paul wrote in the book of Corinthians, "I passed on to you what was most important and what had also been passed on to me. Christ died for our sins, just as the Scriptures said" (1 Corinthians 15:3 NLT). Another well-known Scripture tells us that if we confess our sins, God is faithful and He will forgive us our sins (1 John 1:9). There are no qualifications, no sin listed that cannot be forgiven. We clean the slate or, in modern-day language, "press delete" when we confess our sins to God with a sincere heart. God forgives us and He cleanses us. How wonderful to be able to start over with a clean page. "But if we walk in the light as He is in the light, we have fellowship with one another, and the blood of Jesus Christ His Son cleanses us from all sin" (1 John 1:7).

I walk daily in the light—in the truth of the Bible and my conscience. If I feel the conviction of the Holy Spirit, I confess my wrongdoing and ask Him to help me. What I confess mostly is the sins of my heart—

when I become aware of a negative attitude about a situation or when I put myself in the position of God and judge someone. 1 Peter reads, "and his Spirit has made you holy" (1 Peter 1:2 NLT). The New King James Version uses the word *sanctification*. This is the process that the Holy Spirit is working in us. We are holy and righteous because of the blood of Jesus. There is also a process in walking it out. In daily living I do sometimes sin, and then I have to cleanse my heart; that is the sanctification process that the Holy Spirit is working in me. I can at any time appropriate the blood of Jesus. It was not a cheap price Jesus paid for us, but if the Holy Spirit convicts me, I repent and appropriate the blood of Jesus. Forgive me, Jesus; wash me clean, Holy Spirit—and then I believe He does it and I let go of those things. There have been times in my life when the Holy Spirit revealed generational sins or iniquities that I needed to deal with. At times a teaching crossed my path that revealed some things or the Holy Spirit brought them to my attention. I don't continuously go and dig out sin. God is faithful; if there is something that needs to be purged out of our lives, He will bring us to the place where we can deal with it. The end result? I have become freer, more joyful, and more at peace. I carry a light yoke, the yoke of Jesus: "For My yoke is easy and My burden is light (Matthew 11:30).

The veil was ripped when Jesus died. The separation between the Holy Place and the Holy of Holies ripped supernaturally from top to bottom. God tore that veil! He removed the separation between Himself and man. What does that mean to you? The separation between you and God has been removed. Jesus paid the price that was required from you with His blood. You just need to receive what Jesus has done. Any person covered with the blood of Jesus can come into the presence of God.

It is so much better to walk in a righteous-consciousness. We have been made righteous (made right with God) through the blood of Jesus. "We are made right with God by placing our faith in Jesus Christ. And this is true for everyone who believes, no matter who we are. For everyone has sinned; we all fall short of God's glorious standard. Yet God, with undeserved kindness, declares that we are righteous. He did this through Christ Jesus when he freed us from the penalty for our sins" (Romans 3:22-24 NLT).

Discovering Jesus

A prophecy in Isaiah about Jesus reveals more than one reason why Jesus came. "But He was wounded for our transgressions, He was bruised for our iniquities; the chastisement for our peace was upon Him, and by His stripes we are healed" (Isaiah 53:5). Jesus died for my personal sins, my transgressions. He also died for the iniquities in my generational family bloodline. Leviticus 16:22 tells us that iniquities are the sins of the fathers. The Bible talks about the fathers eating sour grapes and the children's teeth being set on edge (Jeremiah 31:29). If a person has a dad who was an alcoholic, there is no need to repeat that pattern, but often we see it repeat. Jesus died that we can cut off those repeating patterns of iniquity. A friend told me of a time when he asked a person to draw his family tree; he wrote the problems the different family members had on the diagram. The man could see how alcoholism and divorce repeated in his family. Jesus died for those repeating patterns, so that they don't have to continue. That is the power of the cross.

We are healed through the wounds of Jesus. The blood of Jesus paid the price so that we can be confident that God wants to heal us from our diseases. "Who Himself bore our sins in His own body on the tree, that we, having died to sins, might live for righteousness—by whose stripes you were healed" (1 Peter 2:24). I learned this truth early in my Christian walk. It became my habit to first pray before I went to a doctor, and often I didn't have to go at all. When I struggled with a problem that did not want to budge, I continued to pray and ask God for wisdom. For example, my continuing headaches were caused by certain preservatives in foods. It was not that God didn't want to heal them; there was a bigger picture in the situation that I did not know about. I have learned to press in for an answer. Sometimes God answers quickly, other times it takes longer and it is a journey.

My son saw a beautiful vision about the cross. He saw a field and trees burned down. Then he saw the cross and a light shining from behind the cross. Next, the grass and trees started to sprout and turn green. That is what the cross and the blood of Jesus do. Jesus resurrects and restores the dead areas in our lives. The mandate of Jesus is described in Isaiah 61. He came to heal the brokenhearted, to open the eyes of the blind, to set the captives free. It is a picture from ruins to restoration.

Often life circumstances will try to steal my peace. Situations occur, and I feel burdened or worried. This is not the way God wants me to live. I have learned and am continuing to learn to release my burdens and concerns to Him. "Casting the whole of your care [all your anxieties, all your worries, all your concerns, once and for all] on Him, for He cares for you affectionately and cares about you watchfully" (1 Peter 5:7 AMP).

One day I was praying for a situation in North Korea and I felt a bit overwhelmed. I looked at the many different flags on the walls of the prayer room and thought about the many situations in the world that needed prayer—too many to pray about. Then the Holy Spirit started to show me different people with burdens for different countries and situations. I realized that if every Christian just prayed for the situation that the Holy Spirit showed them to pray for and obeyed what the Holy Spirit told them to do, the job would get done.

Revelation 12:11 tells us the secret—that we will overcome because of the blood of Jesus and our testimony. There is power in the blood of Jesus. I often pray the protection of the blood of Jesus over my family. If a lamb's blood was enough to keep the Israelites from the angel of death, the blood of Jesus is even stronger to protect us from evil.

> "He is so rich in kindness and grace that he purchased our freedom with the blood of his Son and forgave our sins" (Ephesians 1:7 NLT).

Discussion Questions: The Blood of Jesus

1. Write in your own words why the blood of Jesus is so important to us. Use a concordance and write down a Scripture reference about the blood of Jesus. Read some of these Scriptures. Discuss.

___

2. For two thousand years the Israelites walked out a picture of forgiveness of sins by bringing offerings. The priests and high priest could get a little bit closer to the presence of God. Jesus established a new way. How do you feel when you approach God in prayer? Do you feel that He accepts you and loves you?

___

3. "When these things were all in place, the priests regularly entered the first room as they performed their religious duties" (Hebrews 9:6 NLT). We can easily fall into working for God instead of having a relationship with Him and serving Him in thankfulness. What is your motivation when you do things for God or for other people?

___

4. The Day of Atonement was a day of repentance from sin and consecration to God. How often and when should we repent?

___

5. Imagine this. Two white cloths. The one is pure white with no spots on it. The other cloth has dirt and stains on it. When we apply the blood of Jesus in faith, the dirty cloth becomes clean and spotless like the pure white one. Read and discuss 1 John 1:9 and Psalm 51:7.

_____
_____
_____

6. Pondering the Word: Focus on a phrase or verse from Hebrews 10:19-23. The Living Bible describes verse 19 beautifully: "we may walk right into the very Holy of Holies where God is, because of the blood of Jesus" (Hebrews 10:19 TLB).

Chapter 10: The Resurrection of Jesus

"He isn't here! He is risen from the dead!"
(Luke 24:6 NLT).

I have heard that in Russia believers greet each other by saying, "He is risen!" How wonderful! It centers a person's attention on what is important about our faith. Jesus is alive! He conquered death and hell and therefore we have hope (1 Corinthians 15:55-57). Because Jesus is alive, we can have a relationship with Him. A relationship cannot be a relationship if there is no communication between the two people. The relationship with Jesus is one in which we can talk to Him and He can talk to us. Often we don't recognize His voice.

Because Jesus is alive, we have a God who is with us; and His help is just a prayer away. Early in 2013, I walked through the very difficult time of my mother's illness and then her passing away. The night she passed into glory, my brother and I arrived at the hospital ten minutes after she died. When I saw her lifeless body, I could see she was not there anymore. In the weeks that she was in intensive care, although she couldn't respond most of the time, I could see that her spirit was still in her body; I knew she still had life in her body. I could clearly see the difference between life and death when her spirit and soul left her body. There is a spiritual world whether we want to believe it or not and we are eternal souls who have an eternal destiny.

Jesus died on the cross on a Friday afternoon. Joseph from Arimathea, who was a rich man, asked Pilate for Jesus' body to bury Him. Pilate released Jesus' body after a Roman officer confirmed that Jesus had died. Joseph wrapped Jesus' body in a linen cloth and put the body in a cave-like grave with a huge stone rolled in front of the opening (Mark 15:42-46). Early Sunday morning, Mary Magdalene and another Mary went to the grave. Suddenly the ground shook and an angel appeared and rolled away the stone in front of the grave. The women were terrified. The angel told them to not be afraid and then reminded them that Jesus told them that He would rise from the dead (Matthew 28:1-8). The women looked into the grave and saw Jesus was not there. They ran back to tell the disciples.

Peter and John ran to the grave. They saw the linen wrappings that Jesus had been wrapped in lying in the tomb. They saw and they believed what the Scriptures had said—that Jesus would rise from the dead. Then they went home. Mary stayed behind. She was crying. She saw someone behind her and thought it was the gardener. She asked him where she could find Jesus' body. Then He said, "Mary!" She knew that voice! It was Jesus, her Rabbi, her Master, *her* Teacher! He was alive! (John 20:3-17).

Jesus told her not to touch Him. He was on His way to ascend to His Father. Reading this, it struck me that Jesus said, "Mary!" He was so personal with Mary. He knew her. He knew she would be worried that His body was gone, and she didn't know what was going on. Mary Magdalene was the woman whom Jesus set free from seven demons (Mark 16:9). She owed her life to Jesus, and she showed it in her devotion to Him. Jesus was on an important mission to His Father to present His blood in heaven as the perfect offering for sin. "For Christ did not enter into a holy place made with human hands, which was only a copy of the true one in heaven. He entered into heaven itself to appear now before God on our behalf" (Hebrews 9:24 NLT). His mission was important enough that He could have skipped stopping at the grave and just gone to appear before His Father, but He did stop to show Mary all was well. We can have this type of relationship with Jesus. Even though there are seven billion people on earth, He knows you by name. What an amazing God that He can have a personal relationship with every person on this earth who desires such a relationship with Him. Today He is extending that invitation to you to enter into a relationship with Him—a relationship in which He knows you by name, knows your hurts and needs. He already knows everything about you, because He created you. He already knows your thoughts before you think them, so there is no reason to hide them (Psalm 139:1-5). It is very freeing to know that God knows everything. There is nothing you can do to surprise Him. Knowing this, I stop and turn away before I do something wrong or think a wrong thought. I quickly say, "No, not that way," and direct my thoughts to think about what is pure, lovely, and edifying.

Knowing Jesus doesn't mean we won't have challenges. When I was writing my first book, I remember how I felt. I had a prophetic word about writing a book. Doors closed to ministry opportunities that I was involved in. My applications for jobs didn't succeed. Top all that off with my kids graduating and moving to college. I had an empty nest and nothing to do except try to write. I am still amazed when I look back and see how the Holy Spirit guided me. This didn't happen for me until I was in my early fifties. I can remember how many years I cried out to God, feeling He had something for me but not finding it. During those years I went through training, read a lot, helped in many different ministries, and was very involved in the area of prayer for churches and cities. Looking back I can see God's wisdom. I needed to mature spiritually. God needed to grow, prune, and mature me. He needed to ground me securely in His love so that nothing could shake me out of it.

Moses is one of the people in the Old Testament who had a special relationship with God—one that causes me to say, "I want to know God like that." "Inside the tent the Lord spoke to Moses face-to-face, as a man speaks to his friend" (Exodus 33:11 TLB). Covered and cleansed by the blood of Jesus, we can each have a personal, intimate relationship with God. This is what Jesus accomplished for us: "And so, dear brothers, now we may walk right into the very Holy of Holies where God is, because of the blood of Jesus" (Hebrews 10:19 TLB).

What joy! There is a way to approach God that is pleasing to Him. The way is through His Son, Jesus Christ (John 14:6). Jesus said He is the only way to His Father. He didn't even put a price tag on salvation. The psalmist said no one can pay God enough to redeem a soul—not even a million dollars (Psalm 49:7). Redemption is free, but it will cost you your life.

How do we do this? We receive Jesus through faith. We believe in Him with our hearts and tell Him that we believe in Him (Romans 10:9). Jesus died for our sins (the things we do wrong). Who has never exaggerated a story or been impatient or had a bad thought about someone else? Thus as I tell Jesus I believe He is the Son of God, I ask Him to forgive me for the things that I have done wrong. The Holy Spirit might bring specific things to mind; if He does, ask for forgiveness for those things specifically. When you are done, ask Him to fill you with His Holy Spirit. We receive Jesus through faith. Some people say they feel different; they have peace after they receive Jesus. I didn't feel much different; I just had to believe by faith that He saved me. I did feel, at times during worship, His joy in my heart.

> The Resurrection is at the very core of the Christian faith. Inasmuch as the Resurrection can be validated and set forth, Christianity stands or falls. We are the resurrection people; we believe in the resurrection from the dead. If you were to name the four global religions that are based on a personality, not just a code of ethics or philosophical construct, only one of those four has a founder who claimed that He would rise from the dead—and did. There is only one reason we propagate a faith as outlandish as this, only one reason we can claim that God came in the flesh, in the form of a man, and died on a Cross for forgiveness of sin: because the founder came out of the grave and stayed out forever.[18]

When Jesus resurrected Lazarus from the dead, He told Martha, "I am the resurrection and the life. He who believes in Me, though he may die, he shall live" (John 11:25). That is the hope my mom knew in her heart. When she breathed her last breath, her physical body died, but her soul and spirit lived on with God in eternity.

---

18. Allen Hood, *The Excellencies of Christ* (Kansas City, MO: Forerunner Books, 2006), 263.

What was Jesus' resurrected body like? During the forty days after His resurrection, Jesus appeared several times to the disciples and others. One evening the disciples were meeting behind locked doors. Suddenly Jesus stood there among them (John 20:19). The whole group was afraid. Jesus told them that He was not a ghost. Ghosts did not have bodies like He had. He showed them the scars of the nails on His hands and feet. He asked them for something to eat, and they watched Him eat a piece of fish (Luke 24:36-43). From this passage we learn that the resurrected body of Jesus could enter a locked room. He was not a see-through person like a ghost; He had a body. The disciples saw Him eat. They could touch His body. We will receive resurrected bodies just like Jesus'! "For our dying bodies must be transformed into bodies that will never die; our mortal bodies must be transformed into immortal bodies" (1 Corinthians 15:53 NLT). It will happen in a moment with the last trumpet blast (1 Corinthians 15:52).

"How mysterious is this plan that was birthed in the pure heart of the infinite, holy God, a perfect plan begotten by a perfect God—to have a God-man sitting on the throne in government. Have you ever thought that right now, within the Trinity, there is a human body? Oh, what grand bliss! The theandric union—the God-man! At the center of the throne a Lamb dwells, a descendent of David, born from the loins of a Jewish maiden."[19] Jesus, the God-man, was the first to receive a new resurrection body, and He is in heaven with Father God.

The resurrection power of Jesus is not just for one day. "We share in the resurrection power of Christ. His resurrected life indwells every believer, releasing divine might and power unto transformation. The resurrection life of Jesus breaks the power of sin in our lives and makes us into a new creation. There is a new life working in us. The law of sin and death no longer prevails in our mortal bodies. The resurrection power enables us to live the crucified life as it produces a glorious new creation within us. We are supernatural people—resurrection people. We testify to the resurrected Christ who now dwells in us by His Spirit. The workings of Christ and the Holy Spirit are inseparable."[20] His

---

19. Allen Hood, *The Excellencies of Christ* (Kansas City, MO: Forerunner Books, 2006), 90.
20. Ibid., 290.

resurrection power works in us as we allow Him to work. "The Spirit of God, who raised Jesus from the dead, lives in you. And just as God raised Christ Jesus from the dead, he will give life to your mortal bodies by this same Spirit living within you" (Romans 8:11 NLT).

One evening, seven of the disciples went fishing. Jesus stood on the shore, asking them if they caught anything. They didn't recognize Jesus. They answered and said that they hadn't caught anything. Jesus told them to throw the net out on the other side of the boat, and they caught so many fish that the net was filled to overflowing. When they got back to the shore, they saw Jesus had prepared fish and bread for them for breakfast. Peter had denied Jesus the night He was captured. I can imagine how guilty he must have felt. Jesus talked to Peter that morning. He asked Peter if he loved Him. Peter answered, "Lord, You know all things; You know that I love You" (John 21:17). Three times Peter denied Jesus; three times Jesus asked Peter if he loved Him. Three times Peter answered that he loved Jesus. Three times Jesus told him to feed His sheep. Jesus restored the relationship between Himself and Peter. He didn't just go on to heaven and leave His disciples to themselves, saying, "I don't care that Peter feels guilty; he needs to get over that." Jesus appeared to those He loved, those whom He had walked with and had a relationship with during His three years of ministry on earth. He cared about the disciples. When the Holy Spirit was poured out, provision was made that we would never be alone. We might often not be aware that the Holy Spirit lives on the inside of us, but He does and we need to learn to recognize Him and hear His voice.

Jesus also gave us brothers and sisters in the faith so that we might strengthen, help, and encourage each other. As I'm writing this book, my son is visiting our family in South Africa, and he has had some of the worst allergy attacks that he has ever experienced. I happened to text him at those times, and all that I could do, being thousands of miles away, was to pray for him. It made my mother's heart very happy to hear this morning that he felt much better today. Thank You, Jesus, for helping my son; thank You, Holy Spirit, for alerting me that it was time to pray. The Holy Spirit is our Helper (John 14:26).

Jesus gave them last orders before He ascended into heaven. "Therefore, go and make disciples of all the nations, baptizing them in the name of the Father and the Son and the Holy Spirit. Teach these new disciples to obey all the commands I have given you. And be sure of this: I am with you always, even to the end of the age" (Matthew 28:19-20 NLT). In the gospel of Mark, we also read that Jesus said that miraculous signs would follow them: they would drive out demons, speak in new languages, and lay hands on the sick and heal them (Mark 16:15-18).

During the time that Jesus appeared to His disciples, He told them to wait in Jerusalem until the promised Holy Spirit came (Luke 24:49). Jesus said John the Baptist had baptized them with water, but soon they would be baptized with the Holy Spirit (Acts 1:4-5). Life with Jesus was never boring. They never knew what would happen next. He told them many parables that they didn't understand. Before Jesus left, He opened their minds to understand the Scriptures (Luke 24:45).

Jesus left them with the words, "But you will receive power when the Holy Spirit comes upon you. And you will be my witnesses, telling people about me everywhere—in Jerusalem, throughout Judea, in Samaria, and to the ends of the earth" (Acts 1:8 NLT). He raised His arms and ascended into heaven. Witnessing this alone would leave me speechless, and what is this about the Holy Spirit? Two angels appeared and told the disciples that Jesus would one day return in the same way as they saw Him leave (Acts 1:11). It sure was an exciting time—Jesus going to heaven and then two angels showing up. They experienced much in the three years that they walked with Jesus. Can you imagine being one of the disciples? Although Jesus is not on earth anymore, He is calling us to walk with Him and He sent us a Teacher. Open our ears, Lord, that we will hear Your voice, that this same Scripture would be true of us: "Then he opened their minds to understand the Scriptures" (Luke 24:45 NLT).

It sounds like this should be the end of the story, but it isn't. Joyfully the disciples went back to Jerusalem to wait for the promise of the outpouring of the Holy Spirit. Life with Jesus was not predictable and definitely not boring. They spent their time in the temple worshiping

God (Luke 24:53). The disciples preached wherever they went and many miracles were done through them (Mark 16:20).

> The birth of the church is dependent on Christ's resurrection from the dead. Without the empty tomb and the appearances of Jesus, no disciples would have left their fishing boats ever again, and no one would have gathered in the upper room. What took place early on the third day after the crucifixion sealed the beginning of a historic shift in world history.[21]

What looked like the end was actually the beginning. It was the beginning of a movement of disciples of Jesus Christ. The Roman Empire and the Jewish leaders thought the death of the leader would end the movement. Instead it multiplied. Like Jesus said, the kingdom of heaven is like a mustard seed—a very small seed that becomes a huge tree. Exponential growth! He also said the kingdom of heaven is like yeast used to make bread—a little bit of yeast in the bread causes the dough to rise (Matthew 13:31-33). Growth is a kingdom principle. Jesus said, "Be my witnesses!"

---

21. Allen Hood, *The Excellencies of Christ* (Kansas City, MO: Forerunner Books, 2006), 263.

Hermie Reynolds

Discussion Questions: The Resurrection of Jesus

1. Seeing a person as evolving from a speck of dust doesn't give much value to a life. If we do not value ourselves, then we do not see value in other people. Read Psalm 139:13-18 and discuss how we should think about life.

2. Sometimes people think that when they become a Christian their problems will end. Read John 10:10, Romans 8:28, 1 Peter 1:6-9, and 1 Peter 5:7-10. How do we explain seemingly contrary Scriptures of abundant life and suffering?

3. "None *of them* can by any means redeem *his* brother, nor give to God a ransom for him—for the redemption of their souls *is* costly" (Psalm 49:7-8). Every person's soul is very valuable to God. In light of this Scripture, how should we view people and evangelism?

4. Read the verses in which Jesus appeared to the disciples (John 20:19-21; Luke 24:36-43). What differences can you see between the resurrected body of Jesus after the cross, and His earthly body before the cross?

5. We will receive a resurrected body. Read and discuss 1 Corinthians 15:42-53.

_____
_____
_____

6. Ponder the Word: There is great joy for us in the fact that Jesus is alive. Take time to think and pray around a verse or phrase from Matthew 28:1-10.

> "He is not here; for He is risen, as He said. Come, see the place where the Lord lay" (Matthew 28:6).

Chapter 11: The Birth of the New Testament Church

"And with great power the apostles gave witness to the resurrection of the Lord Jesus. And great grace was upon them all" (Acts 4:33).

Day after day, 120 believers gathered together to pray. Peter addressed the group and they chose Matthias as an apostle in the place of Judas. Fifty days after the resurrection of Jesus as the group was gathering in the upper room as usual, suddenly a sound like a roaring wind was heard; it looked like tongues of fire that settled on each person. The Holy Spirit filled them, and they all began to speak in different languages (Acts 1:1–2:4).

The commotion attracted attention from those outside the building, and people came running to find out what happened. There were people from many different nations living in Jerusalem. They were surprised to hear that the disciples were speaking in their own languages. Some thought they were drunk. Peter addressed the crowd and told them it was nine o'clock in the morning, too early to be drunk. They were witnessing the outpouring of the Holy Spirit as prophesied in Joel. "People of Israel, listen! God publicly endorsed Jesus the Nazarene by doing powerful miracles, wonders, and signs through him, as you well know" (Acts 2:22 NLT). Peter continued to testify about the death and resurrection of Jesus. His words brought conviction to their hearts. Peter told them what to do—repent of their sins, turn to God, be baptized in the name of Jesus and receive the gift of the Holy Spirit. Three thousand people were baptized and added to the church on that day (Acts 2:1-41).

That was just the beginning. Holy Spirit power exploded the church. The believers regularly gathered together to listen to the teaching of the apostles and to pray and eat together. "A deep sense of awe came over them all, and the apostles performed many miraculous signs and wonders" (Acts 2:43 NLT). They shared what they had with those in need, and daily new Christians were added to them. What a beautiful birth the church experienced. We see a Holy Spirit explosion and it drew people. It changed hearts, people turned to Jesus, and the fruit of it was kindness, sharing with each other, and helping those who were in need (Acts 2:42-47).

We read wonderful accounts of miracles the apostles did. One day Peter and John went to the temple. A man who was crippled from birth asked them for money as he was carried in. Peter responded that he did not have silver or gold, but he would give him what he had and told the man to stand up and walk in the name of Jesus. Peter took the man's hand, and as the man stood up, his ankles strengthened and he could walk; soon he was leaping and jumping and praising God (Acts 3:1-11). The apostles were confident in the power of the name of Jesus. They knew that name and they knew that Man. He heals and He saves!

When the man got healed, Peter saw the crowd gathering and started to preach about the death and resurrection of Jesus Christ. The priests and Sadducees were upset about this and put Peter and John in jail. Peter and John were questioned by the high priest Annas, Caiaphas, and other priests. They wanted to know by whose power Peter did this miracle. Peter in all boldness stated that the miracle happened in the name of Jesus, whom they had crucified and who rose from the dead. The high priest and other leaders had nothing they could say, because the man who was healed was standing there in the midst of them. Then they ordered the disciples not to speak in the name of Jesus anymore. Peter and John said they had to obey God and could not stop speaking in the name of Jesus. The council finally let them go out of fear that a riot would begin. People were still praising God for the miracle of this man walking after being crippled for more than forty years (Acts 4:1-22). The name of Jesus and the power of the Holy Spirit bring confrontation with darkness. Heaven invades earth. God's kingdom advances, and people are healed and set free. The number of believers grew to five thousand (counting only the men).

We find a beautiful prayer uttered by the apostles in Acts 4:29-30, "And now, O Lord, hear their threats, and give us, your servants, great boldness in preaching your word. Stretch out your hand with healing power; may miraculous signs and wonders be done through the name of your holy servant Jesus" (NLT). The result of this prayer was that the building shook, they were filled with power, and they preached the gospel with boldness. How we need the power of the Holy Spirit today. The apostles walked in Holy Spirit power, and we need to do that too. There was great unity among the believers during this time. They shared everything they had and took care of the poor, even to the point of selling their own belongings and land if there was a need. The apostles continued to preach the death and resurrection of Jesus with great power (Acts 4:31-37).

In the culture of those times, when someone came to a belief in Jesus they were seen as outcasts and rejected by their family. It was a time when one paid a price to follow Jesus. Believers in Jesus helped each other and took care of each other. Many miracles happened. It was also a serious time, a time of awe in the church. A man named Ananias and his wife, Sapphira, sold a piece of property. They gave half the money to the church and said that it was all the money they have received. Peter confronted Ananias and asked him why he lied to the Holy Spirit. Ananias didn't need to sell the property or give the money to the church. When Peter confronted Ananias, he fell to the floor and died. The same happened to his wife (Acts 5:1-11). This was a time when the church leaders were sensitive to the Holy Spirit. The Holy Spirit was very active with them and in the community doing miracles. It was a time of sincerity, a time when the Holy Spirit dealt with falsehood. God has always, and will always, require a sincere heart. It was a time when the believers loved each other and cared about each other.

The high priest and his officials were jealous of the apostles and arrested them and put them in jail. During the night, an angel came and unlocked the prison doors and told them to go and preach in the temple.

The next morning, the apostles were preaching in the temple. When the high priest and his council came, they sent for the apostles. They received the message that the jail was locked and no one was in the prison cell. Then someone came with the news that the apostles who had been put in prison were preaching in the temple. Again they were arrested and told not to preach about Jesus. They gave the same answer—they had to obey God rather than man. Gamaliel stepped in and convinced the council not to kill the apostles (Acts 5:17-42). The situation between the Jewish leaders and those who believed in Jesus was tense. The Jewish leaders were not happy to lose their followers to this man, Jesus, whom they thought they got rid of when He died on the cross. I was touched when I read the last verse in this passage and saw how the apostles rejoiced for being whipped for the sake of Jesus. They considered it an honor to be counted worthy to suffer for the name of Jesus. The Peter who now suffered was quite a different man than the Peter who had denied Jesus. Peter, now filled with the Holy Spirit, was bold, even in the face of danger. He did not flinch from speaking the truth about who Jesus was.

Eventually problems appeared. The Greek-speaking believers complained because the food was not evenly distributed between the poor. The apostles realized they needed help and appointed believers, filled with the Holy Spirit and wisdom, who would oversee this ministry. This would give them more time to focus on teaching (Acts 6:1-7).

The persecution increased in Jerusalem, and Stephen, a man full of the Holy Spirit, was arrested and stoned (Acts 7). A great wave of persecution hit the city. A man named Saul was going from house to house to find believers and throw them into prison. As the believers scattered, the gospel spread too. They told people everywhere about Jesus who died and was resurrected. We read about Philip doing many miracles and setting many free from evil spirits (Acts 8:5-8).

Saul was persecuting believers, causing many to be thrown in jail. He requested letters from the Sanhedrin to go to Damascus to arrest believers there and bring them back to Jerusalem in chains. As he was coming close to Damascus, suddenly a light shone around him and he fell to the ground. A voice spoke to him, saying: "'Saul! Saul! Why are you persecuting me?' 'Who are you, lord?' Saul asked. And the voice replied, 'I am Jesus, the one you are persecuting!'" (Acts 9:4-5 NLT). Jesus told him to go and wait in the city. He would be told what to do. As Saul got up, he realized he could not see. For three days, he remained blind. Then God spoke to Ananias, a believer in Damascus, in a vision. He told Ananias to go to Straight Street. There he would find Saul. God spoke to Saul in a vision as he was praying and showed him Ananias who was going to come and lay hands on him and pray for his eyes to be opened.

Ananias knew who Saul was and asked God if He knew how many people Saul killed. God told him that Saul was the man He chose to take the message of Jesus Christ to the Gentiles (those who were not Jews). He went to Saul, laid hands on him, and prayed for him. Scales fell from Saul's eyes and he was baptized. He started to preach about Jesus to the amazement of many (Acts 9:10-30). We see a complete turnaround in Saul, from aggressively persecuting those who believe in Jesus to preaching Jesus. That is what an encounter with Jesus can do.

As I read what happened in the book of Acts, I think it should be exciting to be a Christian. We should expect God to show up and do things. We should expect God to speak to us and show us visions. In Acts 10 we read about Cornelius, who was a Roman officer who lived in Caesarea. He was a kind man and generous to the poor. One afternoon he was praying to God when he saw an angel in a vision. The angel told him that God had seen his generosity and told him to send men to Joppa and ask for a man called Simon Peter to come to his house. While the men were on their way, Peter went onto the roof to pray. He fell into a trance and saw a sheet being lowered by its corners. In the sheet were different animals, birds, and reptiles. Peter was told to kill the animals and eat. He answered, "'No, Lord,' Peter declared, 'I have never eaten anything that our Jewish laws have declared impure and unclean'" (Acts 10:14 NLT). The voice told Peter not to call unclean what God had made clean. Three times this vision repeated. Peter wondered what it meant.

The three men from Cornelius' house arrived at Peter's house. While Peter was still on the roof, the Holy Spirit told him that three men had just arrived, and they were looking for him, and that Peter should go with them. The three men told them they were sent by a Roman officer, Cornelius. Peter invited the men to stay over and the next morning they went to Caesarea. When they arrived at Cornelius' house, Cornelius fell at Peter's feet and worshiped him. Peter told him he was a person just like them; Cornelius should not worship him. He told them that even though their laws forbid a Jewish person to go into a Gentile home, God had showed him through the visions that he should not consider a Gentile as impure or unclean. Peter preached to them the good news about the death and resurrection of Jesus. As Peter was preaching, the Holy Spirit fell upon those listening and they started to speak in tongues. Peter was surprised that God would give the gift of the Holy Spirit to the Gentiles, but then said there was no reason not to baptize this group, because they had already received the gift of the Holy Spirit (Acts 10). Thus, the church began to receive Gentile believers.

As persecution had spread, the good news of Jesus spread. At first they only shared it with the Jews, but soon they began to preach to others too, and large numbers of people came to believe in Jesus (Acts 11:19-21). Persecution increased, and it caused the believers in Jesus to spread, taking the good news of Jesus with them to many places it wouldn't have gone otherwise. I have learned that even in persecution and difficulties, God has a redemptive plan. I might not see it at the time, but God has worked all things for good in my life—even the things that were meant for evil.

When we look at the early church, we see that they demonstrated what Jesus modeled. "We know what real love is because Jesus gave up his life for us. So we also ought to give up our lives for our brothers and sisters" (1 John 3:16 NLT). There are different ways God asks each one of us to step out of our comfort zones. Some might visit the elderly or volunteer somewhere. I see families receive God's heart to foster or adopt. We often have friends or missionaries stay at our house.

Jesus said, "The harvest truly is great, but the laborers are few; therefore pray the Lord of the harvest to send out laborers into His harvest" (Luke 10:2). We can all become harvesters, no matter where we work or minister. Jesus knows what every person we come across needs, and He knows where they are in their relationship with God. Every encounter a person has with a Christian can either draw them closer to Jesus or push them away. I know that the Holy Spirit knows what each person needs to grow closer to Jesus. He can give us the words to say, and whether they lead the person to Jesus or are seed that someone else will water, the Holy Spirit has the right words for every situation.

I remember when my daughter was two years old and she ended up in the hospital. A lady from a church stopped by and talked to me and asked if she could pray for my daughter. She prayed a simple prayer of healing and ended the prayer by saying that God would get the glory for the healing. Even though we attended church every Sunday, we were not in a church where we saw healing or had any expectation that God still healed. The Holy Spirit used those words that God would get the glory, and I started to think about it. God used it to stir in me a desire to see and experience His move in our lives, to not just have a dead faith. A few simple words can unlock a person's heart and the Holy Spirit has the exact right words. Even if we think we have messed up, He is greater than that. He will guide us to use the word that we do not know will even mean anything to someone else. Those words will be like a key in a lock of another's heart. Just be sincere, care about others, and be real. Even if you just love and encourage a person, not many people do that.

One day I took a friend to the art museum in Cincinnati. I bought something at the museum's store and the lady at the counter told me that if my purchase were more than fifteen dollars I would get the money for the parking back. I just thought, *Well, I already paid for the parking; it doesn't make a difference.* Since the purchase was just over fifteen dollars, she encouraged me, and said, "Just take the cash register slip to that lady and she will give you your money back." It was such a little thing, but I just felt blessed that someone even cared enough to do this. She was probably just doing her job, but she did it in such a way that she blessed me and I felt God's blessing through what she did. We can make a difference in people's lives by the way we treat them. You may be the only Bible someone might read. A living testimony has so much more value than words on a paper. Jesus is not physically here anymore, and we are His hands and His feet through whom He is touching others and helping them.

Discussion Questions: The Birth of the New Testament Church

1. The church was birthed with a Holy Spirit outpouring as prophesied in Joel. What do you think is the role of the Holy Spirit in the church today?

2. The early church shared with each other, fed the poor, and gathered together regularly. How important is compassion, meeting needs, and fellowship to you?

3. What was the main message the apostles preached when crowds gathered before people hadn't heard what their message was about? (Read Acts 4:2, 33.)

4. The apostles ministered in great power. Share a miracle or event that made an impression on you as you read about their ministry (Read Acts 5–6).

5. Jesus told the disciples, "You shall be witnesses to Me in Jerusalem, and in all Judea and Samaria, and to the end of the earth" (Acts 1:8). The gospel didn't spread until persecution came. We tend to be resistant to change until a situation becomes very painful or uncomfortable. Share an example of how God worked in your life to bring change during a difficult situation.

6. Pondering the Word: Spend some time and ponder this Scripture and write down any thoughts you receive about it.

   "But you shall receive power when the Holy Spirit has come upon you; and you shall be witnesses to Me in Jerusalem, and in all Judea and Samaria, and to the end of the earth" (Acts 1:8).

Chapter 12: Jesus, Returning Bridegroom King

> "Let us be glad and rejoice, and let us give honor to him. For the time has come for the wedding feast of the Lamb, and his bride has prepared herself" (Revelation 19:7 NLT).

We find different words in the Bible to describe believers. We are called *children of God*. God is our heavenly Father and we are His children living in dependence on Him, trusting and loving Him just as a small child trusts his father and looks to him for all his needs (John 1:12; Romans 8:16). In John 10 we see the picture of a shepherd and sheep. We are the sheep and Jesus the Shepherd. This shepherd knows His sheep by name, and they know His voice. Jesus protects us like the shepherd protects the sheep. He knows us by name, and we get to know Him. He leads us like a Shepherd would lead and protects His sheep, and we come to know His voice. The Bible also calls us "a chosen generation, a royal priesthood, a holy nation, His own special people" (1 Peter 2:9). When we give our lives to Jesus, we become set apart for God. We decide to live differently, and we become people who pray and work to advance God's kingdom on earth.

The Bible also calls us "sons of God" (1 John 3:1; Romans 8:14, 199). Being a son of God is a position of favor. We can also say daughter of God; it will still make sense. A son or daughter is in a more privileged position than a servant, and they will receive an inheritance. We are also called the "bride of Christ." Jesus told several parables about weddings, and His first miracle occurred at a wedding. In Revelation 19:7 we read about the marriage of the Lamb, and we know Jesus is the Lamb of God. To see ourselves as the bride of Christ can be challenging, especially for men. There is a deeper trust between a bride and bridegroom than between a child and a parent. A bride and groom relationship is a mature relationship, compared to the child and parent where the child simply obeys and follows the parent.

Marriage is the closest relationship that we can have with a person on earth, and it is a picture of the spiritual closeness in our relationship with our heavenly Bridegroom, Jesus. When we receive Jesus, the Holy Spirit comes and lives within us. Our relationship with Jesus is even closer than the relationship we have with a spouse. We cannot be with a spouse every second of every day. The Holy Spirit lives inside of us. He knows everything about us (Psalm 139:1-5). He knows all the answers to every problem we will ever face. We have a 24/7 connection with Him. We might not always be aware of His presence or we may even forget that God's Spirit lives in us, but His desire is that we would turn our attention often to Him and talk to Him. "Live in me. Make your home in me just as I do in you. In the same way that a branch can't bear grapes by itself but only by being joined to the vine, you can't bear fruit unless you are joined with me" (John 15:4 MSG). Yes, in eternity we will be the bride of King Jesus, but here and now we get to practice living in intimacy to our King.

> Your Creator knows that true transformation comes in a relationship where love's torrent covers our sin and makes us lovely in His sight. Just as relationships in the past had the power to wound and scar our souls, downloading lies into our thinking…so a passionate pursuit of the Bridegroom holds the key for the deepest level of change in our personalities. Jesus does not come to scare us into submission, but to woo us into friendship with Him. God delivered His transforming truth and the grace for change in a relational package, the person of His Son. Grace has a face; and His face is smiling.[22]

In Matthew 7, Jesus said many would do miracles in His name, but He would say, "I never knew you; depart from Me" (Matthew 7:23).

---

22. Brian Simmons, *Song of Songs: The Journey of the Bride* (Tulsa, Oklahoma: Insight Publishing Group, 2002), 18.

Jesus was indicating a deeper knowing than just superficial acquaintance. We cannot get to know a person better if we do not spend time with that person. My son went on a mission trip to Thailand. Unbeknownst to him, he was seeking to do something for God. The revelation that he received on this trip was that God desired him to love Him. He was not looking for him to work for Him. If his priorities were right—loving God first—then the works of ministry would flow from that. "And you shall love the Lord your God with all your heart, with all your soul, with all your mind, and with all your strength" (Mark 12:30). Jesus was saying He doesn't want us to do works outside of knowing Him personally and having a relationship with Him. Paul's words in Philippians 3:10 in the Amplified Bible reveals the kind of relationship Jesus desires: "[For my determined purpose is] that I may know Him [that I may progressively become more deeply and intimately acquainted with Him, perceiving and recognizing and understanding the wonders of His Person more strongly and more clearly]." The works of the kingdom should flow out of this intimate relationship.

I have heard this beautifully described by a missionary whose ministry takes care of many orphans. She spends time with Jesus to be filled with His love. During one of those times, she saw herself as a little girl standing with her feet on her Father's feet. As He was walking, she was moving along with Him. She says she is following her heavenly Father. He orchestrates everything and she just goes along for the ride. When we put God first and spend time with Him, we will bear more fruit.

We find several places in the Old Testament where God refers to Israel as an unfaithful wife. In obedience to God, the prophet Hosea married a prostitute, Gomer. Their life and marriage became a picture of Israel's unfaithfulness. Hosea received Gomer back after her unfaithfulness. God was showing Israel His heart toward them. He would forgive their unfaithfulness and receive them back. "'And it shall be, in that day,' says the Lord, 'that you will call Me 'My husband,' and no longer call Me 'My Master'" (Hosea 2:16).

Isaiah also has bridal references: "For your Maker *is* your husband—the Lord of hosts *is* His name" (Isaiah 54:5). We see another beautiful picture of God's heart for Israel in Isaiah 62:4; "Never again shall you be called 'the God-forsaken Land' or the 'Land that God Forgot.' Your new name will be 'The Land of God's Delight' and 'The Bride,' for the Lord delights in you and will claim you as his own" (TLB). This is a picture of how Jesus feels about us. You may feel that God has forsaken you, but when you give your life to Jesus you come under that love canopy described in Song of Songs 2:4: "He brought me to the banqueting house, and his banner over me was love." It may take a while to get out of the mess we have made of our lives, but Jesus can help us turn around any situation and bring us into blessing. "We must discover the glorious, completing love of God. If you are single, you do not have to find a mate to discover love. If you are in a difficult, unfulfilled marriage, you do not have to go outside the boundaries to discover love. If you are a known sinner who has struggled with disgraceful habits and thoughts—there is a love waiting for you that will sweep you off your feet. It comes to us like a kiss from heaven. There are places in your heart that will only be healed by Divine romance…so run into Abba's arms today and abandon yourself to Him!"[23]

As related in chapter three, Jesus revealed Himself to a Samaritan woman next to a well after He had sent His disciples for food. Jesus just asked her for water like it was a common practice. Then He offered her living water which He eventually revealed was of a supernatural nature. Later, Jesus invited everyone who was thirsty to come and drink, referring to the Holy Spirit who was coming.

When my daughter was three years old I let her memorize Scriptures. John 7:38 was one of the Scriptures she learned. I don't think she really understood it though. God moved mightily in my life around that time, and in my ignorance and zeal I just taught her Scripture whether she understood it or not. Later I learned that a person's spirit can respond to Scripture even though the mind doesn't fully understand. One day she came to me and said, "Mommy, I pulled up my shirt and asked Jesus to come into my heart." How precious, to hear a little one thirst for Jesus. Although she couldn't understand everything with her mind, her

---

23. Brian Simmons, *Song of Songs: The Journey of the Bride* (Tulsa, Oklahoma: Insight Publishing Group, 2002), 19.

spirit was thirsting for the living God, thirsting to have a relationship with God, inviting Jesus into her heart. God met her and Jesus gave her spiritual Holy-Spirit-Living-Water.

This secret, the relationship Jesus is inviting us into, He revealed to a despised Samaritan woman. She didn't understand it either. We can understand what Jesus meant. This journey begins with inviting Jesus into our lives, allowing Him to wash us from our sins. It doesn't end there; we can go on, let Him clean up our lives and bring us into a place of abundant life. It is a place in life—one that no matter what the circumstances are or what I go through in life I can have abundant life in the Spirit, joy, and peace in every circumstance (Philippians 4:6-7).

There have been times when I was so overwhelmed by circumstances that I didn't feel His abundant life and joy on the inside. As He cleaned me on the inside—cleaned me from my judgments, hurts of the past, unforgiveness, and depression—the well on the inside opened up. Just as we take care of our bodies, we need to take care of ourselves spiritually. I desire to have a flowing Holy Spirit river on the inside; I do not want a dirty, stagnant pond. Some have experienced a one-time infilling of the Holy Spirit that is often accompanied by a Holy Spirit language. We ask in faith and receive in faith (Acts 2:2-18, 38-39; 10:44-48). I found out that I need to be filled daily. Listening to worship songs often fills my heart with joy. Spending time with Jesus, prayer, and in worship are ways to connect with Him and be filled with His Spirit.

Jesus' first miracle took place at a wedding in Cana in Galilee. In Matthew 22:1-14 we read a parable about a king who invited guests to a wedding banquet for his son. Jesus also told the parable about the ten virgins who went out to meet the bridegroom. The five who were wise took extra oil and the other five ran out of oil. If we look at oil in the Bible, anointing oil represented the Holy Spirit. Also we are told not to hide our lamp under a basket but to let our light shine (Matthew 5:15).

The Living Bible describes this beautifully: "And this is the secret: Christ in your hearts is your only hope of glory" (Colossians 1:27 TLB). It is His Spirit shining through us. If we do not spend time with Him to fill us, we will not have extra oil while waiting for Jesus to return. What happened in the parable in the waiting. They all fell asleep. Suddenly, they heard the bridegroom coming. The foolish virgins ran out of oil and missed the wedding feast. Each one of us must have our own personal relationship with Jesus. Our spiritual condition is our own responsibility. When the Bridegroom, Jesus, returns unexpectedly, we cannot ask others for oil—we have to be ready. In Scripture, the bridegroom said to the foolish virgins, "I don't know you." We have time in this life to get to know and spend time with our heavenly Bridegroom, Jesus. It's important that we take the time to do that.

I never understood Song of Solomon and didn't read it much. In my journey to know Jesus I found a wonderful book by Dr. Brian Simmons, *Song of Songs, The Journey of the Bride,* that opened this book of the Bible to me. It can be interpreted in an allegorical or typological way: "Clearly, this is a story of Jesus loving His bride into maturity. In her weaknesses, in her insecurities, in her failings she is loved. That assurance releases power for transformation. Perfect love will cast out fear—fear that keeps us trapped the way we are."[24]

In the early part of the journey, the maiden says, "I am dark, but lovely" (Song of Solomon 1:5). In our early walk with Jesus, He is still cleaning us up. We feel we're not good enough—too sinful, dark—but He says, "I see the *yes* in your heart, and that is lovely to Me." Nowhere in this world will we experience unconditional love like this. Jesus loves us even when we're a mess, when we struggle, He comes and picks us up from the miry clay and sets us on firm ground (Psalm 40:1-3). He died for us before we got our act cleaned up. He is more committed to see us come to maturity than we even realize. When parents have a baby and the child begins to walk, the parents are delighted in each step of growth and advancement that they see in their child. They don't say, "You fell after the first step today, so we will just give up and quit on you." God knows us much better than we know ourselves. He just wants our hearts to say *yes* to Him, and He will clean up our lives and help us grow and mature.

---

24. Brian Simmons, *Song of Songs: The Journey of the Bride* (Tulsa, Oklahoma: Insight Publishing Group, 2002), Introduction.

"He brought me to the banqueting house, and his banner over me was love" (Song of Solomon 2:4). We have a banner over our lives and on that banner is written *love*. Jesus loves you so much, He gave His life for you. God loves you so much, He sent His Son to redeem mankind and restore our relationship with Him, so that those who come into this relationship will become an eternal bride for His Son.

I have been a Christian for many years and there have been seasons when I felt the presence of God and there have been times when I didn't feel His presence. We live and walk by faith and not by what we feel, though it is great to feel His presence. In our daily lives we often encounter challenges. These can be challenges in relationships, work situations, finances, etc. Everything was going well and suddenly there is a problem. Song of Solomon compares those problems to the foxes that spoil the vineyard.

"Catch us the foxes, the little foxes that spoil the vines" (Song of Solomon 2:15). In this journey of loving Jesus and realizing how much He loves us, we encounter the foxes. Those are situations that steal our joy or cause problems in our relationships. We learn to recognize the foxes and refuse to allow them to steal our joy and peace.

In Chapter 3 the maiden refuses to go with her beloved. There have been times when I said, *"No, Lord the price that I need to pay to do this is too much."* Then I experience a grieving in my spirit and a struggle between my will and God's will. I find myself seeking Him and seemingly not finding Him. "I sought him, but I did not find him" (Song of Solomon 3:2). Jesus is patient and although it felt like He left me, He was taking me on a journey of greater surrender.

"You have ravished my heart, my sister, my spouse; you have ravished my heart with one look of your eyes" (Song of Solomon 4:9). If we can come into the place where we know this is how Jesus feels about us, then nothing will be able to stop us. No amount of persecution will derail us. A love like this will overcome every obstacle. This is the journey you are invited on—deeper into the love of God, to fall deeper in love with His Son.

"Awake, O north wind, and come, O south! Blow upon my garden, that its spices may flow out" (Song of Solomon 4:16). "The north wind is the cold, biting wind of adversity. Does she really want the north wind to blow upon her heart? She is willing to embrace difficult circumstances if they will make fruit grow and His fragrance spread… With an unexpected fierceness, the north wind will one day blow upon every passionate heart. There are some issues of God's training in our lives that can only result from testing and trials…Deep pockets of unperceived pride, self-confidence, anger, and fear will only be exposed by the cold cutting blast of the north wind."[25] The south wind brings the blessing. Just as seasons change, we experiences the adversity of the north wind, and the blessing of the south wind at different times in our lives.

"The watchmen who went about the city found me. They struck me, they wounded me" (Song of Solomon 5:7). In life we will experience situations when we are misunderstood, even persecuted for believing in Jesus. Even if it is not a physical wound, we can be hurt in our spirit/soul. Love for Jesus will bring us through these situations; only love is a strong enough motivation to persevere.

"I *am* my beloved's, and my beloved is mine. He feeds his flock among the lilies. (Song of Solomon 6:3). She is secured in love and follows her beloved to where He is feeding His flock. She is maturing in this journey from a place of receiving and the Holy Spirit working in her life, to a place where she can help to feed His flock and be part of gathering the harvest.

"Who is this coming up from the wilderness, leaning upon her beloved?" (Song of Solomon 8:5). The young woman is coming into maturity. During her struggles she learned to lean. She is now leaning on Jesus and not trusting in her own strength. "Set me as a seal upon your heart, as a seal upon your arm" (Song of Solomon 8:6). The Holy Spirit seals her heart. She is marked for Jesus. He has ownership over her.

---

25. Brian Simmons, *Song of Songs: The Journey of the Bride* (Tulsa, Oklahoma: Insight Publishing Group, 2002), 144-145.

We see the progression of immature love to a life of fruitfulness and being owned by Jesus. Jesus walked in that kind of mature love, doing what He saw the Father doing and not operating from His own strength. This is the journey you and I are on, if we yield and say yes to Jesus.

The wedding feast that is awaiting us is described in Revelation 19. The voice of a great multitude is heard praising and worshiping God. "Praise the Lord! For the Lord our God, the Almighty, reigns. Let us be glad and rejoice, and let us give honor to him. For the time has come for the wedding feast of the Lamb, and his bride has prepared herself" (Revelation 19:6-7 NLT). When Jesus returns, He will gather His bride for a wedding feast. I noticed the Scripture reads that the bride of Jesus has made herself ready. There is a working together, a yielding to the Holy Spirit in the process of getting ourselves ready to meet Jesus.

This is the relationship Jesus, the Son of the living God, is inviting you into. It starts with surrendering our lives to Jesus and asking forgiveness for our sins, but that is just the beginning of this exciting relationship. You can go as deep as you would like to go. There is no limit and no end in this journey. We sell ourselves short and settle for second best if we just receive Jesus as Savior and then do not continue to pursue Him with everything in us. No earthly relationship, no amount of money or things would ever compare to running wholeheartedly after Jesus. It will bring surprises along the way, but I have found that He always knows best and He has my best interests in mind. I want to invite you into this pursuit. You will not be disappointed. I cannot guarantee that you will not have heartache and trials, but by accepting Jesus, you have the One on your side who will help you to overcome any situation. I cry out with Paul, "Oh, that I might know Him!" (see Philippians 3:10).

How do I enter into a personal relationship with Jesus?

The Holy Spirit will stir your heart as you read this book. He will show you where He desires you to change. The process begins with realizing that you cannot live a life good enough to be accepted by God; in your own strength you will never be able to do it. You can pray from your heart or pray along with the prayer below. If the Holy Spirit brings specific things to mind as you pray, talk to God about them. If it was something you did wrong, take it to the cross and ask forgiveness (Romans 3:23). Don't rush through this time of prayer; be sensitive to pause and listen to what the Holy Spirit brings to your mind and talk about those things with God. Remember the Holy Spirit convicts of sin, but if you just sit in condemnation, that is not His desire. The blood of Jesus can wash us clean from any sin (Psalm 103:12). If He leads you afterward to ask someone you wronged for forgiveness, know that this will bring freedom as those relationships are mended and restored.

Prayer for Salvation

> Jesus, I come to You and I surrender my life to You (Matthew 22:37). I know I cannot be good enough or live a life good enough to be accepted by You. I bring every situation and heart attitude when I have not been able to live up to Your standards of holiness to the cross. Forgive me, Lord, for trying to be the lord over my own life. Forgive me for the things that I have done wrong—when I have hurt others or myself, didn't tell the truth, or have not acknowledged You. Cleanse me, Holy Spirit (1 John 1:9). Set me free to serve You.
>
> I receive You, Jesus, as the Lord and King over my life (Romans 10:9-10). Come, Holy Spirit, and fill me with the love, joy, and peace of God. Fill me to overflowing. (If you feel the presence of God as you're praying, pause and wait a bit and then continue.) Thank You that You have filled me and are indwelling me by Your Holy Spirit (Luke 11:11-13; John 7:38-39).
>
> Thank You, heavenly Father, that You are now my heavenly Daddy, the One who takes care of me and helps me. Thank You, Holy Spirit, that You are now present in my heart and that I have a Helper to lead and guide me, a Teacher who will open up the Scriptures to me, and an Advocate who will fight on my behalf.

Discussion Questions: Jesus, Returning Bridegroom King

1. Share your thoughts around this quote: "Just as relationships in the past had the power to wound and scar our souls, downloading lies into our thinking…so a passionate pursuit of the Bridegroom holds the key for the deepest level of change in our personalities."[26]

2. Love is a much better motivator than law. You will do more for someone you love than for a stranger you do not know. Read Psalm 91:14. What is the key to deliverance in this Scripture?

3. What did Jesus mean when He shared this with the woman at the well? Give an example if you can think of one. "If you only knew the gift God has for you and who you are speaking to, you would ask me, and I would give you living water" (John 4:10 NLT) (Read John 7:38.)

---

26. Brian Simmons, *Song of Songs: The Journey of the Bride* (Tulsa, Oklahoma: Insight Publishing Group, 2002), 18.

4. We read about the parable of the ten virgins in Matthew 25:1-13. How do we prepare so that we will have extra oil ready when our Bridegroom, Jesus, returns?

_____
_____
_____

5. Heaven is not only for eternity. When we walk with Jesus, we can experience tastes of heaven here on earth. We can be filled with the joy and peace of Jesus. We can feel His love. Read Zephaniah 3:17. What do you learn about God's feelings from that Scripture?

_____
_____
_____

6. Pondering the Word: Pick one of the following passages and focus on God's love for you: Psalm 23, Isaiah 54:10, Song of Solomon 2:10-16 or 4:12-16.

Pondering the Word

This is an exercise to dialogue with God about a specific Scripture or Scripture passage.

Make the Scripture personal. What does God want to say to me through this Scripture? How does it connect to my life?

Guidelines:

- Confidentiality: If someone shares a personal issue that God is speaking to them about, it stays in the group.

- No counseling: This is not a time for counseling or the giving of advice. It is a time for each person to seek God and hear from Him personally.

- This is not a time to focus on the history of a verse unless the Holy Spirit leads you there. It is a time for God's Word to speak personally to you.

- Remember we are all practicing. Don't stress out. Don't try to figure out whether these are your thoughts or God's thoughts. His voice sounds the same as our thoughts; the longer you walk with Him the more you will be able to discern His voice. If you're just beginning this journey, go with the thoughts that come to you first unless they don't agree with the Bible. God can speak to you through pictures in your mind or just a word or a phrase; sometimes He brings back a situation or a different Scripture that connects with this one. I write down the impressions. Sometimes they are like puzzle pieces, and in the end they make sense. If my thoughts are very random, I take my thoughts captive in the name of Jesus to come under the obedience of Jesus Christ (2 Corinthians 10:4-5).

Structure:

Allow fifteen to thirty minutes for journaling and listening to the Holy Spirit. Remember, no stress. I have at times just sat with my eyes closed, allowing the Holy Spirit to minister to me through the Scripture. For example, "let the peace of God rule in your hearts" (Colossians 3:15). Every time I say the words in my mind, the Holy Spirit ministers God's peace to my heart. I wasn't writing anything. It is a Holy Spirit time—if you don't feel like writing, it is a time of freedom to allow God to lead you, to sit, to write, to read, to pray the Scripture back to Him. Enjoy it.

At the end, if there is time, the leader can ask who would like to share how they have experienced this time.

The leader can ask if anyone needs prayer and orchestrate the prayer time how he or she feels best—to close with prayer and include the prayer requests or to individually pray for someone. Be sensitive to the Holy Spirit. You want the group to be a safe place and the person who receives prayer to be blessed, strengthened, and encouraged.

"The Spirit of the Lord is upon Me, because He has anointed Me to preach the gospel to the poor; He has sent Me to heal the brokenhearted, to proclaim liberty to the captives and recovery of sight to the blind, to set at liberty those who are oppressed; to proclaim the acceptable year of the Lord" (Luke 4:18-19).

About the Author

Hermie Reynolds and her husband, John, live in Hamilton, Ohio, and have four grown children. She taught in a public school until she had children, and then she and her husband led the children's ministry in their church in South Africa for ten years. In 1999, they moved to Cincinnati, Ohio. She has since taught many classes about the attributes of God, and prayed for the Cincinnati region for more than ten years, at the Cincinnati House of Prayer. John and Hermie are part of the Oxford Vineyard Church planting team. Hermie's first book, *Discovering God*, was released in 2013.

Hermie can be contacted at hermiereynolds@gmail.com or visit www.DiscoveringGod.info.

More Titles by Hermie Reynolds

Discovering God
by Hermie Reynolds
$14.95
ISBN: 978-1-936578-73-3

We live in a time where we see natural disasters like never before. These things cause us to ask questions. Reading this book will bring greater understanding about the way God works. It is designed to be used individually or in small groups. Each chapter has discussion questions which will help you dig deeper into the Scriptures and apply what you learned to your life and situation.

More Titles by 5 Fold Media

Beauty Treatments
by Jodie Dye
$16.95
ISBN: 978-1-936578-63-5

Esther was a young Jewish girl, chosen because of her great beauty to be part of King Xerxes' harem. In preparation for meeting him, she received twelve months of beauty treatments.

Jodie Dye consecrated herself in a similar manner for a different king: King Jesus. As she studied the book of Esther, she discovered many spiritual truths for herself. Applying these *Beauty Treatments* will challenge you, unlocking the inner radiance only available through a closer relationship with the King of Kings.

Apples, Brownies, or Both?
by Kathy Hill
$25.95
ISBN: 978-1-936578-80-1

In this devotional cookbook, Kathy Hill teaches you how to eat healthy and still enjoy your favorite foods. You can escape the diet trap and start experiencing lifelong health without saying goodbye to the world of goodies.

Kathy shares delicious, healthy recipes for everything from main dishes to tempting desserts, as well as numerous practical tips for staying on track with your health journey. Follow along with Kathy as she shares her struggles and victories in her own health journey.

Like 5 Fold Media on Facebook, follow us on Twitter!

"To Establish and Reveal"
For more information visit:
www.5foldmedia.com

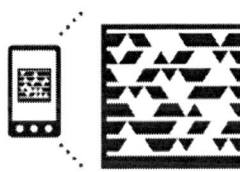

Use your mobile device to scan the tag and visit our website.
Get the free app:
http://gettag.mobi

CPSIA information can be obtained
at www.ICGtesting.com
Printed in the USA
FFOW03n0334201014
8104FF